Spread
Yourself Thin

Spread Yourself Thin

More than 140 Delicious, Low-Fat, Easy Recipes for Every Occasion

Wendy and Barb

HarperCollins*Publishers*Ltd

Photographer: Caroline Ryan/Dickens Street Studio
Food Stylist: Mara Subotincic
Make-up: Janice Shantz
Props Stylists: You-Neek Designs
Props generously donated by Bowrings (Burlington), Pier 1 Imports
(Oakville), Laura's Ladies' Wear (Burlington), and Stokes (Burlington)

First edition

Canadian Cataloguing in Publication Data

Buckland, Wendy
Spread yourself thin : more than 140 delicious low-fat, easy recipes for
every occasion

Includes index
ISBN 0-00-638666-0

1. Low-fat diet - Recipes.   I. Nicoll, Barb.   II. Title.

RM237.7.B82 1997   641.5'638   C97-932327-4

98 99 00 WEB 10 9 8 7 6 5 4 3 2 1

Printed and bound in Canada

To think that we change people's lives through a healthier lifestyle is a wonderful way for us to live our lives. Best wishes in all that you do.

Wendy and Barb

Contents

Introduction

You asked for it. You've got it. Special delivery from the kitchens of Wendy and Barb, straight to you.

Time and again you came up to us at events, sent us reams of faxes and bags of letters, saying you wanted a cookbook, Wendy and Barb style. We listened. We loved the idea. And here it is — *Spread Yourself Thin.*

Over and over you asked us, how do you eat? What do you eat? What do you eat when you have a couple of kids, a job, a picky spouse? What do you do at Christmas, birthdays, Thanksgiving? What do you eat when you love food and have a life?

Hey, that's us. Our world is a pressure cooker, too, but we also devote as much time as we can to having fun with family and friends. Parties are one of our favorite things around. But we found a way to play and eat well, and still lose 38 pounds in Wendy's case, and 65 pounds for Barb. And we have kept it off.

You asked us to write a cookbook, but to keep it fun. You want fun? Check out the Aphrodisiac Spread. Keep it simple, you said. No problem, these recipes are fast and easy, yet delicious, gourmet fare. We've included lots of news you can use, snippets of weight-loss and healthy eating information that will help you munch your way lean. Can you have a drink? You bet. We've included a cocktail section at the beginning of each spread with a recipe for a before-dinner sip. We often have a glass of wine with dinner, so we've even added our recommendation for wines we love. Since you can't have a great evening without music, we've each chosen our favorite CD to match the theme of the various spreads, great to listen to as you cook and to play during the meal. And it's all because we believe being fit, healthy and achieving a sensible weight should be tons of good fun.

When we were losing weight, we often wished for a cookbook like *Spread Yourself Thin*, something lively and informative that paid tribute to people like us, people who love to eat. Writing this book has helped plug that gap, and that's how we've approached so many things since we started turning our personal battles of the bulge into a growing business aimed at helping millions of over-weight people.

Back then, when we couldn't find the low-fat, good-tasting food we wanted on store shelves, we got busy and made it ourselves. Today, you can find our line of "You Won't Believe This Is Low Fat" Skinny Dips on store shelves across North America. Barb is a choco-holic. You don't get to weigh 198 pounds loving carrots. But why, oh why couldn't she find ready-made, low-fat, chocolate baked goods that tasted yummy, gooey good? Was she asking too much?

Apparently, yes, according to the baked goods industry. So we made our own. Bikini Brownies are just as accessible as the chocolate bar at your grocery checkout. And that's what we wanted. You can take them home, eat them with 1% low-fat ice cream all smooshed together in a bowl and still feel good about yourself.

It's not fair that you have trouble finding low-fat, good-tasting foods in your local market. We have told people from the beginning, "Speak up." Tell your store manager you want these items, or you'll pull your business and shop somewhere else. For the average Canadian, that works out to about $10,000 for a year's worth of groceries. You bet your Bikini Brownie that store manager is going to help. We kept pushing for low-fat foods and are proud to say we were the squeaky wheels who helped bring many low-fat packaged foods to Canadian store shelves.

Too often, though, people complain that the lower-fat foods cost more than their artery-clogging cousins. Yes, it's true. And no, it's not fair. But before you refuse to pay that extra money, take a moment and think about this. We spend so much money on our hair, cosmetics, clothes with that special label, yet we don't care about what we eat. Spend the 50 cents more to get the low-fat cheese. Aren't you worth it?

It's not an easy transition to make. We didn't used to think we were worth it, either. Wendy started her journey of self-discovery first. A single mom, owner/operator of a small hair-dressing salon who had battled both rheumatoid arthritis and kidney disease, she found herself weighing 168 pounds on a five-foot-four-inch frame. A perfect size 16.

Then, one night, while flipping through *Muscle & Fitness* magazine, maybe just like you're flipping through this book right now, the answer came like a bolt from the heavens through a reader's testimonial. Wendy's eye was caught by the story of a woman who had beaten her arthritis pain by eating a sensible, low-fat diet combined with weight training to build muscle and strengthen her joints. At age 37, Wendy was re-born. Today, in her forties, fit and fabulous, Wendy weighs 130 pounds, is strong and healthy and loves to share her story, just as she did a couple of years ago when a client who was so miserable about all the weight she gained after the birth of her son, Jake, asked Wendy how she changed her life. Could she do it, too? That unhappy mom was Barb, who drank up all of Wendy's knowledge and experience the way she used to suck back milkshakes. From the start, the attitude was "I can do this." Did she do it, you ask? This five-foot-seven-inch gal, who used to tip the scales at close to 200 pounds, today weighs a trim 132 and runs marathons. She can even keep up with four-year-old Jake, and that's saying something.

Now that you've heard a bit about us, you understand that we were average Canadian women with a pretty typical problem — fat. No surprise then that we have made it our personal mission to wipe out heart disease and obesity in Canada. Tall order, you say? Hey, we've never listened to anybody who told us something was impossible before. Why start now?

When we embarked on our weight loss, we found our friends and families started treating us like we had some sad ailment called "diet-itis." Now, as you probably gathered, we are two ladies who love to party. Friends and family mean the world to us. Yet, suddenly, the invitation well dried up. What gives, we wondered. Turned out, people thought they couldn't ask us if they were having a pool party or an office picnic. We were "on diets." What would they serve us, a plate of twigs?

It never occurred to anybody that they could actually whip up delicious creations that were low in fat and calories. Not fat-free — our bodies need some fat. We just don't need to go over that magic 30% fat mark.

So we did what we always do when faced with a brick wall. We went through it. Yep, Wendy and Barb started throwing some pretty awesome parties. Our maiden voyage was a bash for Jake to celebrate his first birthday. And the guests couldn't get enough of the delicious food. We even made a low-fat birthday cake. People actually took food home, but only after they also begged us for the recipe. We knew then that no matter what high-fat situations people might throw at us, we could come up with low-fat solutions and serve up a meal that would make anybody proud.

Every birthday, every golf function, every Saturday night, every

Grey Cup or Super Bowl, even every romantic dinner for two, everything that happens every day of the year is covered in this cookbook. When you go to a party, take a platter of appetizers from this book, or some of our Skinny Dips. Ask the host or hostess if you can bring dessert and wow them with a little something from *Spread Yourself Thin*. Make the meal fit your life, instead of the other way around.

Being fit and thin is great, but that isn't what it's all about. It's about feeling good about you. You are your own person now. Suddenly, it becomes easier to accept things about your body and love it, yes actually love it. We still get misty when people come up to us at seminars and tell us how we have helped change their lives. It means so much to us to pass on what we have learned. Knowledge kept to yourself is knowledge wasted.

That's why we're so thrilled to be able to bring our message to TV with our syndicated show. We want as many people as possible to know that we have a way of eating that will last for life. This is no short-term diet. Sure, those work for awhile, but then you're right back where you started. No, we want you to start living a whole new way, for yourself. One of the benefits will be that you will lose weight. But beyond that, you will gain control. You just won't want to eat the old "fat" way when this tastes so good and gets such fabulous results. No choice required. Drop that fat-packed cocktail weenie and get into some of our delicious nibbles like Smoked Salmon Cigars, Cozumel Crunch Crackers, Crab and Artichoke Tartlets. Get the picture?

We are the happiest we have ever been in our entire lives. We eat well, and it's fun eating. We still have our glasses of wine, and fit in our exercise, and we wake up each morning knowing no matter what life hands us, we're up to the challenge.

We are not models. We were not born with these physiques. But we learned how to shop for the food we needed to eat to be healthy, how to keep our bodies active and, most of all, how to love ourselves.

The last part of the equation was discovering how to eat healthy and well every single day of the year, even the special events and holidays. We hit the kitchen and used our imaginations. We adapted high-fat classic recipes for the way we wanted to eat today. And now we want to share that with you. This is the food from our table. Make it for the people you love. And, of course, that includes you.

Chapter 1

Elegant Soirée

Menu

How Swede It Is Swedish Meatballs
Stuffed Mushroom Caps
Basic and Herbed Yogo Cheese
Lori s Skinny Shrimp
Smoked Salmon Cigars
Mesclun Greens with Champagne Vinaigrette
Light and Luscious Watercress Soup
Black Tie Chicken
Elegant Pork Tenderloin
Moroccan Couscous Delight
Magic Baked Potatoes
Roasted Asparagus
Sinful Cherries Jubilee
Angelic Chocolate Cake with Devilish Raspberry Sauce

Introduction

It's always amazed us that people think they have to cook and serve high-fat meals to impress their company, that special date, or their partner on a rare night when Grandma takes the kids. And it's just not true.

We came up with many of these recipes in the early days of our weight loss, when people assumed that if we were limiting our fat intake, we were eating twigs, dirt and the occasional cabbage leaf. "We can't have Wendy and Barb over. They're on a diet."

It's not the fat and calories that make the meal. In fact, we challenge anybody to dig into Lori's Skinny Shrimp, our savory Stuffed Mushroom Caps or rich and satisfying Magic Baked Potatoes and be able to identify them as anything other than yummy gourmet fare.

The key is to make food fun, to experiment and to learn how to make substitutions to turn high-fat food bombs into figure-saving delights. We make it our motto that nobody leaves our dinner parties feeling hungry, guilty or fat. And you bet we serve a glass of wine, too.

We always get a kick out of putting on feasts based on the recipes found in this Elegant Soirée Spread. Nobody believes that delicious Elegant Pork Tenderloin, silky Light and Luscious Watercress Soup and sumptuous smoked salmon rolled around our own version of skinny cream cheese we call Yogo are all low in fat and calories. And don't forget to save room for dessert. Isn't it great to hear that at last!

So light the candles, put on some music and pour the wine.

Check out our recommendations for tunes and tipples coming up next and in every chapter. Welcome your guests. And relax. You've just spread yourself a thin, guilt-free Elegant Soirée.

♼ Cocktails
Kir or Kir Royale

With its lovely color, served in fluted glasses next to a tray of cocktail nibbles like mini pita breads and our You Won't Believe This is Low Fat Skinny Dips, this drink is a classy way to start a special meal.

The difference between Kir and Kir Royale is that the first calls for white wine and the second uses Champagne. Some people believe you're wrecking the Champagne by adding the sweet black currant-flavored syrup, but nothing compares with that lovely, festive sparkle. Go ahead. Buy a less expensive brand of the fizzy stuff and spoil yourself and your guests.

> 1/2 oz (10 mL) cassis (black currant) syrup or liqueur
> 4 oz (125 mL) dry white wine, sparkling wine or Champagne

Pour cassis into a Champagne flute and top with wine.

Make a Toast

You'll have to do it sometime. From a simple "cheers" with friends to more formal occasions, a toast is a warm and wonderful way to begin an evening. The etiquette can be complicated, but the rule of thumb is to look the person you are toasting in the eye as you sip. The host generally toasts a guest, but the guest should respond. Keep it short, strive for charm and, above all, be genuine. If you suspect you'll be called on and you're nervous, then practice. Memorize a quote or a quip and use that.

Wine Suggestions

Sparkling wine or Champagne

Music Picks

From Wendy

Celine Dion, *The Colour of My Love*. Columbia.

From Barb

Natalie Cole, *Stardust*. Elektra.

Weight Out the Fat

Here's a formula to blitz off fat and build calorie-burning muscle. Cut fat to 20 grams per day at the same time you pick up weights for 2 hours a week. Get a proper program at a local gym and stick with it. Remember, the more muscle on you, the more efficient the metabolism inside.

Serves 8

**Per serving
(4 meatballs):**

**Calories: 205
Fat: 7 g**

How Swede It Is Swedish Meatballs

Nobody will be asking "Where's the beef?" when they tuck into these low-fat cousins of the traditional cocktail party treat.

**1 3/4 lb (875 g) ground turkey
1 egg white
1 medium apple, peeled and chopped very fine
1/2 onion, chopped very fine
1/3 cup (75 mL) bread crumbs
1 tbsp (15 mL) grated fresh ginger
salt and pepper to taste**

**Mustard Sauce:
1/2 cup (125 mL) apple jelly
1/2 cup (125 mL) Dijon mustard**

Preheat oven to 400°F (200°C).

Put the ground turkey in a large bowl and add the egg white. Add the apple, onion, bread crumbs, ginger, salt and pepper to the turkey mixture. Mix well and form into small meatballs. Put meatballs on a non-stick cookie sheet and bake for about 15 minutes until cooked through. Drain on paper towels and keep warm.

Mustard Sauce: In a small saucepan, heat the apple jelly and mustard over medium heat. Stir frequently and cook just long enough to combine ingredients and heat through. Do not boil.

To serve, arrange meatballs on a platter and serve sauce on the side for dipping or put meatballs directly in sauce and toss. Serve in a large bowl with toothpicks.

Stuffed Mushroom Caps

Makes about
20 appetizers

Per appetizer:

Calories: 32
Fat: 1.2 g

These savory little devils can be served as an appetizer, or they make an elegant side dish for a simple main course such as grilled chicken or fish.

> 1 lb (500 g) medium-sized mushrooms
> 2 tsp (10 mL) olive oil
> 1 cup (250 mL) finely chopped onion
> 2 cloves of garlic, minced
> 1 tbsp (15 mL) chopped fresh basil
> 1 tbsp (15 mL) chopped fresh rosemary
> 1/2 cup (125 mL) chopped fresh parsley
> 1/2 cup (125 mL) bread crumbs
> salt and pepper to taste

Wipe the mushrooms with a damp tea towel to remove any dirt. Remove the stems and chop them finely.

Preheat oven to 450°F (230°C).

Heat the oil in a skillet and add the onion and garlic. Cook over low heat until lightly browned, about 5 minutes. Add the mushroom stems and cook for an additional 3 minutes. Add the basil, rosemary, parsley, bread crumbs, salt and pepper. Sauté another 3 minutes, then set aside to cool slightly.

Place the cleaned mushroom caps on a non-stick baking sheet and fill each with equal amounts of the stuffing. Bake for 15 to 20 minutes or until stuffing is nicely browned. Serve immediately.

Makes 1 cup
(250 mL)

Per serving
(1tbsp/15 mL):

Calories: 15
Fat: trace

Basic and Herbed Yogo Cheese

Here it is, our secret weapon! For all of you who say creamy, fatty things are your diet downfall, Yogo was sent straight from heaven to make sure you win the war on fat. Keep a batch in the fridge, flavor it however you like, use it like we do as an ingredient in dozens of recipes and you'll never want cream cheese again.

Basic Yogo Cheese:
2 cups (500 mL) plain non-fat yogurt (no fillers
   like gelatin or tapioca)

Place yogurt in a coffee-filter-lined colander set over a bowl. Let stand in refrigerator overnight. Discard any liquid that accumulates in bottom of bowl. This procedure can be repeated to achieve a firmer "cheese."

Herbed Yogo Cheese:
Basic Yogo cheese
1 tbsp (15 mL) chopped fresh parsley
1 tbsp (15 mL) chopped fresh chives
1/4 tsp (1 mL) salt
1/2 tsp (2 mL) freshly ground pepper
hot red pepper sauce to taste (optional)

Put Basic Yogo cheese in a bowl. Add the remaining ingredients and mix well. Form mixture into a loaf shape and place on a platter. Garnish with whole chives. Serve with your favorite crackers or bread sticks.

Lori's Skinny Shrimp

Serves 4

Per serving:

Calories: 153
Fat: 1.7 g

Take it from us, Lori knows from skinny. Wendy's buff and beautiful sister, also a former size 16, is always a big hit at parties when she walks in with a platter of these rosy delights.

> 2 tbsp (30 mL) Old Bay seasoning
>   (available at most specialty food shops)
> 1 cup (250 mL) water
> 1/2 cup (125 mL) white vinegar
> 1 1/2 lb (750 g) medium shrimp, shelled and
>   deveined

Combine all the ingredients, except shrimp, in a saucepan. Bring to a boil and add the shrimp. Cook for about 2 minutes, or until shrimp are opaque. Drain and serve warm with cocktail sauce and lemon wedges, if desired.

The Skinny on Shrimp

Don't overcook, or you'll have a dish of shrimp-flavored erasers!

Serves 8

Per serving:

Calories: 165
Fat: 2.5 g

Smoked Salmon Cigars

Don't worry, these cigars are good for you. We just love smoked salmon. It's a luxurious treat that is guaranteed to make your dining companions feel special. And remember, any leftover slices of fish freeze beautifully, but wrap them up well.

> juice of 1 whole lemon
> 2 to 3 drops Tabasco sauce
> freshly ground pepper to taste
> 1/3 cup (75 mL) chopped fresh parsley
> 1/2 lb (250 g) smoked salmon, thinly sliced
> 1 recipe Yogo cheese (see page 14)
> 1 tbsp (15 mL) chopped fresh dill

Put the lemon juice, Tabasco, pepper and parsley in a shallow dish. Add the salmon and marinate for 30 minutes.

Put Yogo cheese in refrigerator and let it stand overnight again to produce a firmer "cheese."

Mix the dill with the Yogo.

To assemble, top a slice of salmon with about 1 teaspoon (5 mL) Yogo. Roll it up like a cigar and secure with a toothpick. Arrange on a serving platter and garnish with lemon slices and additional fresh dill sprigs, if desired.

Mesclun Greens with Champagne Vinaigrette

Serves 6

Per serving:

Calories: 15
Fat: trace

For all those people who ask if we have to live on salad, we say, "Of course not." But having a plate of this elegant greens mixture on the side is a welcome addition to any spread. And the sweet-savory Champagne dressing is oh-so-California chic.

> 6 cups (1.5 L) mixed baby lettuces
>   or mesclun mix
> 1/4 cup (50 mL) Champagne or
>   Champagne vinegar
> 2 tbsp (30 mL) strawberry preserves
> 1 tbsp (15 mL) vegetable oil
> 2 tbsp (30 mL) vegetable broth
> salt and pepper to taste

For dressing, combine the Champagne, preserves, oil, broth, salt and pepper in a container with a tight-fitting lid. Shake well to combine and refrigerate until ready to use. At serving time, drizzle over the greens and toss. Garnish with a few pine nuts or slivered almonds, if desired.

The Skinny on Greens

You've probably noticed at your local grocery store all the interesting greens that are now available. You can buy them mixed in bulk or washed and pre-torn in bags. They are excellent products and very convenient. Or choose two or three unusual ones and make your own unique combination.

Light and Luscious Watercress Soup

Nobody will miss the cream in this surprisingly rich-tasting soup. If you can't find watercress, you can use spinach, but do try to find the cress. It has a wonderful, peppery flavor that blends well with the parsley.

> 2 tsp (10 mL) soft margarine
> 1 onion, chopped fine
> 2 tbsp (30 mL) all-purpose flour
> 2 1/4 cups (560 mL) vegetable broth
> 1 12-oz (375 mL) can evaporated skim milk
> 2 cups (500 mL) fresh parsley sprigs
> 2 cups (500 mL) watercress sprigs
> 1/8 tsp (0.5 mL) freshly grated nutmeg
> salt and pepper to taste

Melt the margarine in a non-stick skillet. Add the onion and cook over medium heat for about 5 minutes. Sprinkle the flour over the onion and cook for 2 minutes, stirring constantly, until fully incorporated and smooth. Slowly stir in the broth and milk and bring to a boil, stirring constantly with a wire whisk. Lower heat to a simmer and add the parsley and watercress. Add the nutmeg, salt and pepper to taste. Cover and cook for 5 minutes.

Drain the soup in a sieve set over a bowl. In a blender, combine all the solids left in the sieve and 1 cup (250 mL) of the cooking liquid. Purée for 30 to 40 seconds. Return mixture to the pan and add the remaining cooking liquid. Heat through and serve immediately.

Black Tie Chicken

Serves 4

Per serving:

Calories: 285
Fat: 6 g

The Normandy region of France brings us dishes that feature tart apples, vinegar and heavy cream to make sauces for pork and poultry. Sounds good to us, but the cream's gotta go. We took the basic flavors, substituted heart-healthy, low-fat yogurt and came up with a real oo-la-la gourmet sensation.

2 tart apples (such as Granny Smith), cored
   and chopped
2 red peppers, cut in large dice
1 onion, chopped
1 1/2 cups (375 mL) apple juice
1/4 cup (50 mL) apple cider vinegar
salt and pepper to taste
2 tsp (10 mL) olive oil
4 boneless, skinless chicken breasts
1/4 cup (50 mL) non-fat sour cream

Dredging mixture:
2 tbsp (30 mL) all-purpose flour
1/4 tsp (1 mL) salt
1/4 tsp (1 mL) pepper

In a non-stick skillet, combine the apples, red pepper, onion, apple juice, vinegar, salt and pepper. Bring mixture to a boil, then reduce heat and simmer for about 5 minutes.

Combine the flour, salt and pepper on a plate.

In a non-stick skillet, heat the oil. Dredge each breast in the seasoned flour mixture, shaking off excess, then add to the pan. Cook for about 3 minutes. Turn the chicken over and cook another 3 minutes until both sides are nicely browned and cooked through. Add the apple mixture to the chicken and bring back to a boil. Reduce heat and simmer for about 10 minutes. Remove chicken to a serving platter and keep warm. Stir the sour cream into the apple mixture and just heat through. Do not boil. Pour sauce over chicken and serve.

The Skinny on Garlic

One of our favorite appetizers is a simple roasted whole head of garlic. Roasting the garlic makes it soft and taste sweet and almost nutty. Sort of like us. Just trim the top eighth of an inch (2 mm) or so off the whole head of garlic (leave the skin on), sprinkle 1 teaspoon (5 mL) of olive oil over the top, wrap in foil and pop in a 350°F (175°C) oven for about 40 minutes. Squeeze the garlic onto toasted slices of baguette. Yum.

Elegant Pork Tenderloin

Serves 4

Per serving:

Calories: 200
Fat: 5 g

Low-fat recipes always seem to make you miss out on the crunchy, crispy finishes to cooked meats and poultry. No fair, we say. Good fare, we want. Here's a delicious pork roast with a crusted coating that will satisfy anybody looking for some well-browned, crusty crunch.

> 5 cloves garlic, minced
> 1 tsp (5 mL) dried thyme
> 1 tsp (5 mL) freshly ground pepper
> 1 tbsp (15 mL) chopped fresh parsley
> 1 tbsp (15 mL) lemon juice
> 1 tsp (5 mL) olive oil
> 1 lb (500 g) pork tenderloin

Preheat oven to 450°F (230°C).

Line a shallow roasting pan with aluminum foil and coat lightly with cooking spray. In a small bowl, combine the garlic, thyme, pepper and parsley. In a separate bowl, combine the lemon juice and oil.

Brush the tenderloin with the lemon and oil mixture and rub garlic mixture over the top, pressing lightly to help it adhere. Place the tenderloin in the prepared pan, crusted side up. Bake for 20 to 30 minutes or until center of tenderloin is no longer pink. Remove from oven and let stand 10 minutes. Carve into 1/2-inch (1 cm) slices.

Serves 8

Per serving:

Calories: 263
Fat: 4.1 g

Moroccan Couscous Delight

Couscous came to North America from North Africa, where it is served with most meals. Made from fine-grained semolina, each grain separates into a lovely, fluffy mound of individual little pearls when cooked. It's the texture that makes couscous so wonderful. It's fat-free and delicious. If you've never tried it, give it a go. We think you'll love it.

> 1 tsp (5 mL) olive oil
> 1 1/2 cups (375 mL) finely chopped onion
> 1 1/2 cups (375 mL) frozen peas
> 2 tbsp (30 mL) chopped fresh sage
> 2 tbsp (30 mL) chopped fresh parsley
> 1 tsp (5 mL) dried marjoram
> 2 cups (500 mL) vegetable or de-fatted chicken broth
> 2 cups (500 mL) couscous
> salt and pepper to taste

In a non-stick skillet, heat the oil. Add the onions and sauté for about 8 minutes, until softened and lightly browned. Add the peas, sage, parsley, marjoram, broth and couscous. Cover and cook over low heat for 5 minutes or until couscous has absorbed the liquid. Add salt and pepper to taste and toss couscous lightly with a fork. Transfer to a serving dish and serve immediately.

The Skinny on Marjoram

If your oregano jar is bare, no problem. Marjoram makes a good substitute, and vice versa. Just remember to use about half the required amount of oregano when it's standing in for marjoram.

Magic Baked Potatoes

Serves 8

Per serving:

Calories: 150
Fat: 2 g

"These aren't low-fat!" We get that all the time when we serve these guys. Trust us, they really are good for you and your guests. And nobody but you, and the jeans you couldn't fit into before, will know. That's what makes them magic.

>   4 large baking potatoes
>   2/3 cup (150 mL) low-fat cream cheese
>   1/2 cup (125 mL) non-fat sour cream
>   1/4 cup (50 mL) skim milk
>   2 tsp (10 mL) vegetable oil
>   2 tbsp (30 mL) minced garlic
>   1/2 cup (125 mL) finely chopped onion
>   3 tbsp (45 mL) chopped fresh parsley
>   salt and pepper to taste

Pierce the potatoes with a fork and bake in a 350°F (180°C) oven for about 1 hour. When cool, slice them in half lengthwise and scoop out the pulp into a bowl, being careful not to tear the skins. Add the cream cheese, sour cream and milk and beat with an electric mixer until well combined. No mixer? A potato masher will do in a pinch.

Heat the oil in a non-stick skillet. Add the garlic and onion and sauté until tender. Add the parsley, salt and pepper and stir to combine. Add skillet mixture to potatoes in the bowl and mix well. Stuff the potato mixture back into their shells and place them on a baking sheet. Bake for an additional 10 to 15 minutes or until heated through.

Roasted Asparagus

You can boil it, steam it, why not roast it? Asparagus tastes terrific no matter how you serve it, but we find this way makes it a bit sweeter, the flavor a tad more intense and the color becomes an even richer deep green. It just looks so pretty on your table, you might throw away your steamer for good.

> 1 lb (500 g) fresh asparagus, ends trimmed
> 1 tsp (5 mL) olive oil
> 1/2 tsp (2 mL) chopped fresh rosemary
> 1 clove garlic, minced
> 1/4 tsp (1 mL) salt
> pepper to taste

Preheat oven to 500°F (260°C).

Put the asparagus in a large plastic bag. Add the oil, rosemary, garlic, salt and pepper. Seal the bag and shake to coat asparagus with oil. Put the asparagus on a non-stick baking sheet and roast for about 10 minutes until asparagus is "tender-crisp."

Clockwise from top:
Stuffed Mushroom Caps (p. 13)
Mesclun Greens with Champagne Vinaigrette (p. 17)
Magic Baked Potatoes (p. 23)
Angelic Chocolate Cake (p. 26)
Black Tie Chicken (p. 19)
Smoked Salmon Cigars (p. 16)
Light and Luscious Watercress Soup (p. 18)

Sinful Cherries Jubilee

Serves 12

Per serving:

Calories: 240
Fat: 4.8 g

We know you love chocolate because we do, too. To this day, Barb can't get enough of our sinful-tasting Bikini Brownies. Well, hold on to your bikinis, because we found a way to make chocolate go one better on the decadent scale: Cherries Jubilee.

> 1 package (490 g) Wendy and Barb's Bikini Brownies
> 1/2 cup (125 mL) granulated sugar
> 1 tbsp (15 mL) cornstarch
> 2 tbsp (30 mL) water
> dash of salt
> 2 cups (500 mL) pitted sweet cherries, cut in half
> 2 tbsp (30 mL) cherry liqueur
> 6 cups (1.5 L) low-fat vanilla frozen yogurt

Cut brownies into 12 pieces. In a saucepan, combine the sugar, cornstarch, water and salt. Cook over medium heat until mixture starts to thicken, stirring constantly. Add the cherries to the pan and reduce heat. Simmer for 3 to 5 minutes. Take the pan off the heat and stir in the cherry liqueur. When ready to serve, place a brownie on a serving plate, top with 1/2 cup (125 mL) frozen yogurt and spoon warm cherry sauce over it.

Clockwise from top:
Old Fashioned Ham (p. 62)
Mocha Madness Chocolate Cake (p. 70)
Drunken Fruit (p. 56)
Sharp and Sweet Salad (p. 60)
Saintly Scalloped Potatoes (p. 65)
Blueberry Muffins (p. 57)

Serves 12

Per serving:

Calories: 135
Fat: 1 g

Angelic Chocolate Cake with Devilish Raspberry Sauce

You'll feel full of the devil when you tuck into this light and elegant dessert. But no need to pay for your sins. We're talking 1 gram of fat and about 150 calories for cake and sauce. This is heaven!

> 1 cup (250 mL) sifted cake and pastry flour
> 1 1/4 cups (425 mL) granulated sugar
> 1/3 cup (75 mL) unsweetened cocoa powder
> 1/2 tsp (2 mL) salt
> 12 large egg whites, at room temperature
> 1 1/2 tsp (7 mL) cream of tartar
> 1 tsp (5 mL) vanilla

Preheat oven to 325°F (160°C).

In a bowl, sift together the flour, 3/4 cup (175 mL) of the sugar, cocoa and salt.

In a second bowl, beat the egg whites until foamy. Add the cream of tartar and continue beating until soft peaks form. Slowly add 1/2 cup (125 mL) sugar while beating and continue until the egg whites form stiff peaks. Beat in the vanilla and sprinkle the remaining 1/2 cup (125 mL) sugar over the egg whites. Gently fold in.

Very gently fold the flour mixture into the egg whites. Pour the batter into a 10-inch (25 cm) tube pan.

Please Note: Do not use a non-stick tube pan and do not grease the pan.

Bake for 45 minutes or until a toothpick inserted in the center comes out clean. Invert the pan and let the cake cool. Transfer cake to a cake plate and serve with Devilish Raspberry Sauce (see next page).

The Skinny on Chocolate Syrup

Nobody loves chocolate more than we do and, boy, were we happy to find out chocolate syrup has just 73 calories and less than half a gram of fat per 2-tablespoon (30 mL) serving. Wow! Drizzle over 1% ice cream. Swirl on a caramel rice cake for a real treat. Or just lick it off a spoon when you need a fix. But just one!

**Makes 1½ cups
(375 mL)**

**Per serving
(2 tbsp/30 mL):**

**Calories: 32
Fat: 0 g**

Devilish Raspberry Sauce for Angelic Chocolate Cake

1 10-oz (300 g) package of frozen raspberries
1/4 cup (50 mL) granulated sugar
1 tsp (5 mL) fresh lemon juice
1 tsp (5 mL) grated lemon zest

In a blender, purée the raspberries, sugar and lemon juice. Strain the sauce through a fine sieve to remove seeds. Put the sauce in a serving dish and sprinkle it with grated lemon zest to garnish. Refrigerate until ready to serve.

Chapter 2

Aphrodisiac Spread

Menu

Be Still My Artichoke Hearts Dip
Caviar-Stuffed Cherry Tomatoes
Rockin Oysters Rockefeller
Oh You Teaser Caesar Salad
Veggie Nibblers
Get Lucky Pasta
Decadent Roast Chicken with Figs
Exotic Herbed Orzo
Garlic Smashed Potatoes
Succulent Lemon-Parsley Vegetables
Sweet Sin Chocolate-Dipped Fruit
Erotic Ambrosia Parfaits

Introduction

W e'd like to have this delicious spread every Saturday night. Well, maybe not *every* Saturday. Oh, why not? We deserve it. And so do you.

Everybody needs a little spice in their life, so we came up with the idea for the Aphrodisiac Spread. Each recipe, from Get Lucky Pasta to Erotic Ambrosia Parfaits, has at least one ingredient that folklore claims puts a tiger in your tank.

Among the foods that some say can get you in the mood faster than a Barry White festival are asparagus, ginger, coriander, lemons, onions, garlic, hot peppers, honey, milk, eggs, ginseng, oysters, shellfish — well, you get the idea. Actually, we think just about any food can be an aphrodisiac if you're in the mood for love. And don't forget chocolate!

The natural time to serve some of these recipes would be when you and your mate are enjoying a quiet night, just the two of you, over a candle-lit table, some sexy music and a bottle of wine. But why not have a few couples over for a lighthearted "theme" dinner? Celebrate life and love. Maybe you can even pair off a few singles. Do you tell what the evening's theme is? Can you keep it a secret until the next day when your guests start phoning to say thanks?

Being good scientists, we did the research into aphrodisiacs to design these recipes. And although we're not making any claims, some of these dishes sure turned up the heat a notch or two when we tried them out. Now it's up to you to see if what they say about foods like oysters and garlic is true.

The best thing about these recipes is they're all low in fat and calories, so if one thing leads to another, you won't feel bogged down by a huge meal. And remember, lovemaking is a great way to burn off calories!

♉ Cocktails

The martini may be making a fashionable comeback, but to us it never went away. It's got to be the sexiest drink on the planet, served in chilled stem glasses to be sipped and savored. It's sophisticated, glamorous and guaranteed to make your guests (or guest) feel very special.

Your pre-dinner cocktail should be respected and anticipated just like the meal itself. Have just one, and make it a special experience. As our guest bartender Torsten "Hoss" Drees says, "Have just one drink. Yes, there's no fat in alcohol, but there are calories, and also we're not promoting drinking to excess." And remember, the calories in alcohol are "empty calories," meaning they have no nutritional value, so keep it to a single cocktail.

The classic martini is gin and dry vermouth. The amount of vermouth varies, depending on how dry your guests like their drinks. We went to Mike Chisolm, general manager of the Keg Restaurant in Toronto, service manager Ben Rutherford and Area Manager Drees for a lesson in proper martini making, and got quite an education. Thanks to all.

The Keg crew suggests making your martini mixing an event for you and your guests. Have them gather around your bar or kitchen counter. Custom-make each drink. Very dry, you say? You can even use a plant sprayer to merely mist the glass with the vermouth. Be dramatic. Hold it at arm's length. Set out your olive and lemon twist garnishes and play superstar bartender to the hilt.

Here's the recipe for the classic, plus a few Keg variations we call "fun-tinis" for your guests to try.

The Classic Martini

1/8 to 1/4 oz (2 to 5 mL) dry vermouth
3 oz (60 mL) premium gin or vodka

Pour the vermouth and gin into a cocktail shaker with lots of ice. Stir, don't shake. Strain into a chilled glass and garnish with a lemon twist or olive.

Monkey Business

1 1/2 oz (35 mL) vodka
1/4 oz (5 mL) banana liqueur
1/4 oz (5 mL) Malibu rum
Splash of pineapple juice

Mix all the ingredients over ice in a cocktail shaker. Shake. Pour over ice. Garnish with pineapple wedges.

The Scarlet

1 1/2 oz (35 mL) vodka
1/2 oz (10 mL) cassis
1/2 oz (10 mL) cranberry juice

Mix all the ingredients in a shaker over ice. Place a lime twist, made from a thin strip of lime peel cut with a knife and twirled around your finger, into a chilled glass. Pour drink over.

The Melancholy

1 oz (20 mL) vodka
1/2 oz (10 mL) Amaretto
1/2 oz (10 mL) melon liqueur
1/2 oz (10 mL) cranberry juice

Shake all the ingredients in a cocktail shaker over ice. Pour into a chilled glass, garnished with a lime twist.

Blue Over You

1 oz (20 mL) vodka
1 oz (20 mL) blue Curacao
splash of lime juice
splash of Grenadine syrup

Put all the ingredients in a shaker with ice. Shake and strain into a chilled glass. Garnish with a lime twist.

The Aztec

1 peperoncini (Italian red pepper)
1 1/2 oz (35 mL) vodka
1 1/2 oz (35 mL) Commemorativo Tequila

Slit the tip of the pepper with a knife and slip it on the rim of a chilled glass. Mix the vodka and tequila in a cocktail shaker filled with ice. Strain into a glass.

Chocolate Mousse Martini

shaved chocolate
2 oz (50 mL) vodka
1 oz (25 mL) dark crème de cacao

Fill a chilled glass with ice and top with shaved chocolate. Mix the vodka and crème de cacao in an ice-filled cocktail shaker and pour over ice.

The Decadent Martini

1 wedge of lime
1 1/2 oz (35 mL) Absolut Kurant vodka
1 1/2 oz (35 mL) Cointreau

Run the lime wedge around the rim of a glass. Fill with ice and squeeze the lime over. In a cocktail shaker, mix vodka and Cointreau over ice. Pour into a glass.

Wine Suggestions
Gamay or our favorite, Pisse Dru

Music Picks

From Wendy

Barry White, *The Icon Is Love*. A&M.

From Barb

Luther Vandross, *Your Secret Love*. Epic.

Choosing the Wine

Can't decide which wine matches your favorite pasta sauce? While we believe anything goes, there are certain vino-pasta marriages that are made in heaven. Here are some suggestions:

Low-fat cream: Chardonnay or Chenin Blanc
Meat: Valpolicella
Seafood: Orvieto, Chardonnay
Tomato: Chianti or Zinfandel
Primavera: Beaujolais

Be Still My Artichoke Hearts Dip

Serves 6

Per serving:

Calories: 23
Fat: 0.2 g

Artichokes contain a natural ingredient that makes everything you eat after them taste slightly sweeter. And that includes smooching your honey. Try a batch of this silky dip and see if you can taste the difference.

> 1 19-oz (540 mL) can white beans, such as
> cannellini, drained
> 2 garlic cloves
> 3 tbsp (45 mL) fresh lemon juice
> salt and pepper to taste
> 2 tbsp (30 mL) chopped fresh parsley
> 1 14-oz (398 mL) can artichoke hearts, drained
> 4 green onions, sliced

Preheat oven to 350°F (180°C).

In a food processor or blender, process the beans, garlic, lemon juice, salt and pepper to a smooth consistency. Spoon it into a bowl and add the chopped parsley, artichoke hearts and green onions. Mix gently and put into an oven-safe casserole dish. Bake, uncovered, for 10 to 15 minutes until heated through. Serve warm with crackers or baked tortilla chips.

Makes 24

**Per serving
(1 tomato):**

**Calories: 7
Fat: 0.2 g**

Caviar-Stuffed Cherry Tomatoes

Caviar is an exquisite aphrodisiac, conjuring up images of decadent excess, Champagne and glamor. Serving a platter of these colorful, elegant appetizers is guaranteed to turn up the heat.

> **24 cherry tomatoes, red, yellow or combination
> of both
> 1/2 cup (125 mL) non-fat sour cream
> 1 oz (25 g) red salmon caviar
> fresh dill for garnish**

Wash the tomatoes and cut off the stem end. Hollow out the pulp and seeds with a small spoon and turn the tomatoes upside down on paper towels to drain.

   With a small spoon, fill the tomatoes with sour cream and top with a small amount of caviar. Cut small sprigs of dill and garnish each tomato with a sprig. Arrange on a serving platter.

The Skinny on Fads

What's "in" as far as we're concerned?

1. Loving food.
2. No guilt.
3. Truth in labelling.
4. Exercise, because it feels good and makes you look great.
5. Salsas, hot sauces, herbs and fresh foods bursting with taste.

What's "out"?

1. Feeling guilty about food.
2. Counting calories.
3. Compulsive exercise.
4. Fad diets.
5. Blah, fat-free food with no taste, no inspiration and no hope.

Rockin' Oysters Rockefeller

Makes 24

Per serving (1 oyster):

Calories: 14.6
Fat: 0.5 g

The classic. Oysters. These sensual delights slip down your throat to melt even the hardest heart. The traditional version of this dish contains bacon, butter and cream. We turned to a dash of Parmesan and the licorice flavor of the sexy French aperitif, Pernod, to jazz up our recipe. With just 14 calories each and a trace of fat, these treats will rock your world.

> 8 oz (250 g) fresh spinach leaves
> 1 tsp (5 mL) soft margarine
> 3 green onions, chopped
> 2 tbsp (30 mL) chopped celery leaves
> 2 tbsp (30 mL) chopped fresh parsley
> 1/2 cup (250 mL) bread crumbs
> 1 tbsp (15 mL) grated Parmesan cheese
> 1 tbsp (15 mL) Pernod
> 24 large oysters, scrubbed, opened and cleaned
> coarse sea salt

Preheat oven to 425°F (220°C).

Cook the spinach in a saucepan for 3 or 4 minutes over medium high heat until wilted, using just the water clinging to the leaves after washing. Drain well and chop very fine.

Melt the margarine in a non-stick saucepan. Add the spinach, green onions, celery leaves, parsley, bread crumbs, Parmesan and Pernod. Cook over low heat for 3 to 4 minutes. Set aside.

To open an oyster, lay it on a damp tea towel, insert the flat part of the shell facing up and the hinged end toward you. Put the tip of a small knife into the gap in the hinge and twist the knife until the hinge releases. Slide the knife along the inside of the upper shell and open oyster. Discard top shell and check oyster meat for any broken shell.

Put enough sea salt on a baking sheet to make a bed for the oysters so they don't tip. You may need two baking sheets. Place the oysters in the half shell onto the salt and spoon a little of the prepared stuffing onto each. Bake for 6 to 8 minutes until hot and bubbly. Serve immediately.

The Skinny on Salad Dressing

Looking for a new way to thicken salad dressings without oil or mayo? Try fruit pectin. It comes in liquid or powder, has no flavor and, although it's usually used to make jams and jellies "set," it works just as well to thicken dressings. Stir in the powder, adding a bit at a time until you get the consistency you want. Be careful. It won't take much.

Oh You Teaser Caesar Salad

Serves 6

Per serving
(1 cup/250 mL):

Calories: 194
Fat: 7 g

Garlic ranks high on the aphrodisiac list, and there's no better way to enjoy it than in creamy, garlicky Caesar Salad. We left out the eggs, and most of the oil from this dressing, using the broth and Dijon mustard to produce the creamy smooth texture that makes a Caesar such a pleaser.

> 2 tbsp (30 mL) Dijon mustard
> 2 anchovy fillets, patted dry and finely chopped
> 2 tbsp (30 mL) olive oil
> 1/3 cup (75 mL) fresh lemon juice
> 1 tsp (5 mL) grated lemon zest
> 1/3 cup (75 mL) vegetable broth
> 4 cloves garlic, minced
> 6 cups (1.5 L) romaine lettuce washed, dried and
>   torn
> 1/3 cup (75 mL) Parmesan cheese
> freshly ground black pepper

To make dressing, combine in a jar with a tight-fitting lid the mustard, anchovies, oil, lemon juice, lemon zest, broth and garlic. Cover and shake well. Refrigerate until ready to use.

Put lettuce in a large bowl and pour dressing over. Add the Parmesan and pepper to taste. Toss and serve.

Makes about 30

**Per serving
(4 pieces):**

**Calories: 52
Fat: 0.5 g**

Veggie Nibblers

Finger food is sexy food. Make up a tray of these savory little nibbles and feed them to each other one at a time. Bet you don't finish the veggies.

> 2/3 cup (150 mL) bread crumbs
> 2 tbsp (30 mL) Parmesan cheese
> 1 egg white
> 1 tsp (5 mL) water
> 1 cup (250 mL) sliced zucchini
> 1 cup (250 mL) sliced yellow squash
> 1 cup (250 mL) cauliflower florets
> salt and pepper to taste

Preheat oven to 400°F (200°C).

In a plastic bag, combine the bread crumbs and the Parmesan.

In a bowl beat the egg white and water until frothy. Dip a few of the vegetable pieces at a time into the egg white then put them in the bag with the crumbs and shake gently until coated. Repeat with remaining vegetables. Place them on a non-stick baking sheet and bake for about 10 minutes until nicely browned.

Serve with a fresh tomato salsa, if desired. Also great with one of Wendy and Barb's "You Won't Believe This Is Low-Fat" dips.

Get Lucky Pasta

Serves 4
Per serving:
Calories: 378
Fat: 6.5 g

We're not making any promises, but there's something about the mix of certain aphrodisiac foods that tends to send romance meters into the red. Not only does this dish contain sensual scallops, it also has time-honored love potions like clam juice, garlic and basil (the Italians swear this herb is a guaranteed *amore* jolt) all served on elegant angel hair pasta for a carbo boost that is sure to keep lovers busy all night.

> 1/2 cup (125 mL) bread crumbs
> 8 oz (250 g) angel hair pasta
> 3 tsp (15 mL) olive oil
> 1/2 cup (125 mL) chopped fresh parsley
> 1 tsp (5 mL) dried basil
> 1 clove garlic, minced
> 1/2 tsp (2 mL) dried oregano
> 1 tbsp (15 mL) all-purpose flour
> 1 8-oz (250 mL) bottle clam juice
> 1 lb (500 g) sea scallops, cut in 1/2-inch
>   (1 cm) pieces
> salt and pepper to taste

Spread crumbs on baking sheet and toast at 400°F (200°C) for 3 to 5 minutes. Cook the pasta according to package directions.

While pasta is cooking, heat 2 teaspoons (10 mL) of the oil in a non-stick skillet. Add half of the parsley, the basil, garlic and oregano. Sauté over medium heat for 1 minute. Add the flour and cook for 1 minute more, stirring constantly. Slowly add the clam juice and stir constantly until sauce thickens. Turn down heat to very low.

Heat the remaining 1 teaspoon (5 mL) of oil in a non-stick skillet. Add the scallops and cook quickly, about 4 minutes, stirring occasionally. Do not overcook. Drain the pasta, add sauce and scallops and toss gently. Sprinkle the remaining parsley and bread crumbs over the top to garnish and serve.

The Skinny on Garlic, Part 2

Next time you roast a chicken or some veggies, toss a handful of unpeeled garlic cloves into the pan. When supper is done, take out the cloves and squeeze out the lovely, mild garlic. Put it in with your gravy, mashed potatoes, or just on its own.

Decadent Roast Chicken with Figs

Serves 4

Per serving:

Calories: 304
Fat: 4.2 g

Is it the voluptuous shape of the fig that makes it an aphrodisiac, or some mysterious natural ingredient we don't yet know about? A serving of this sumptuous main course might help further your research.

> **4 boneless, skinless chicken breasts**
> **1/4 cup (50 mL) minced garlic**
> **1/4 cup (50 mL) vegetable broth**
> **1/2 tbsp (7 mL) dried oregano**
> **3 tbsp (45 mL) red wine vinegar**
> **3 tbsp (45 mL) capers**
> **2 bay leaves**
> **1/4 cup (50 mL) brown sugar**
> **1/2 cup (125 mL) white wine**
> **5 fresh figs, cut in quarters**

Combine the chicken, garlic, broth, oregano, vinegar, capers and bay leaves in a shallow dish. Cover and refrigerate at least 6 hours or overnight.

Preheat oven to 350°F (180°C).

Arrange the chicken breasts in a baking dish and pour the marinade over. Sprinkle the sugar over each breast and pour the wine over top. Put in oven. After 15 minutes of cooking, add the figs to the chicken. Bake for about 1 hour, basting occasionally with marinade. Arrange chicken on serving dish and pour sauce over. Don't forget to toss out the bay leaves.

Exotic Herbed Orzo

Orzo is a wonderful little pasta shape that looks like rice at first, but has the unmistakable sexy slip of pasta. It makes a striking side dish.

> 1 tsp (5 mL) soft margarine
> 1 onion, finely chopped
> 1 clove garlic, finely minced
> 1 cup (250 mL) orzo pasta
> 3 cups (750 mL) vegetable stock
> 1/4 cup (50 mL) chopped fresh basil
> salt and pepper to taste

In a non-stick skillet, melt margarine and add the onion and garlic. Cook over medium heat until softened. Add the orzo and cook, stirring, until pasta is lightly browned. Add the stock and cook, stirring occasionally, over low heat for about 10 minutes. Drain any excess broth and stir in basil. Season with salt and pepper.

Garlic Smashed Potatoes

Serves 8

Per serving:

Calories: 100
Fat: 1 g

Garlic is another one of those Top Ten entries on the aphrodisiac hit parade. These rich and creamy taters get a boost from a hit of garlic, but don't be put off by the number of cloves in the recipe. Boiling them removes much of garlic's intensity and leaves a wonderful flavor.

    4 large potatoes
    6 cloves garlic, peeled but left whole
    1/4 cup (50 mL) skim milk
    1/2 cup (125 mL) non-fat sour cream
    salt and pepper to taste

Peel the potatoes and cut them in 1-inch (2 cm) cubes. Put the potatoes and garlic in a saucepan and add enough cold water to just cover. Bring to a boil and cook over medium heat for 10 to 15 minutes until tender. Drain well, then mash the potatoes and garlic together with a potato masher. Don't be too enthusiastic — they should look "smashed" as opposed to smooth. In a saucepan, heat the milk over medium heat for 1 to 2 minutes. Add to the potatoes along with the sour cream, salt and pepper. Mix well and serve.

The Skinny on Feeling Full

Ever wonder why a portion of one food fills you up, but others leave you feeling hollow? Australian researchers at the University of Sydney found it's what you eat, rather than the size of the portion, that dictates how you feel after noshing. The best choices to feel full longer? Potatoes, oatmeal. oranges, apples, bread and popcorn (low-fat, please) do the trick.

Succulent Lemon-Parsley Veggies

If you're going to enjoy all the dishes in our Aphrodisiac Spread, and the fun that follows, you'd better eat your veggies!

> 2 tsp (10 mL) olive oil
> 2 carrots, sliced
> 1/2 lb (250 g) asparagus, cut into 1 1/2-inch (3 cm) pieces
> 1/2 lb (250 g) mushrooms, wiped and cut in half
> 2 cloves garlic, finely minced
> 3/4 cup (175 mL) vegetable broth
> 1 cup (250 mL) drained artichoke hearts
> 1/4 cup (50 mL) chopped fresh parsley
> 1 tbsp (15 mL) fresh lemon juice
> 1/2 tsp (2 mL) dried thyme
> salt and pepper to taste
> 2 tbsp (30 mL) Parmesan cheese

Heat the oil in a large non-stick skillet. Add the carrots, asparagus, mushrooms and garlic. Sauté over medium-high heat for 5 to 7 minutes.

Add the broth and artichoke hearts and bring to a boil. Lower heat and simmer for about 5 minutes. Add the parsley, lemon juice, thyme, salt and pepper, and simmer an additional 5 minutes until all vegetables are tender. Put the vegetables in a serving dish and garnish with additional parsley and lemon slices. Sprinkle with Parmesan.

Sweet Sin Chocolate-Dipped Fruit

Serves 1

Per serving:

Calories: 169
Fat: 3.9 g

What's an Aphrodisiac Spread without chocolate? This recipe makes a single serving, but you can always share. That's what love is all about. This recipe also doubles or triples easily to feed more guests. As a real eye-popping treat, dip those huge California strawberries, leaving the stems on.

> 2 tbsp (30 mL) pure semi-sweet chocolate chips
> 2 tbsp (30 mL) skim milk
> 1 piece of fruit such as:
>   sliced apple
>   sliced pear
>   sliced banana
> 2 large slices of pineapple
> 4 large strawberries
> Use your imagination!

In a small saucepan over low heat, melt the chocolate with milk, stirring constantly until smooth and well-mixed. Remove from heat and dip fruit into chocolate mixture. Place on a waxed paper-lined baking sheet and chill until firm.

Serves 4

Per serving:

Calories: 173

Fat: 1 g

Erotic Ambrosia Parfaits

The sweet mix of tropical fruits and coconut takes us straight to a romantic, palm-studded island and a hammock for two beneath the stars.

> 2 tbsp (30 mL) shredded sweetened coconut
> 2 seedless oranges, segmented
> 1/2 cup (125 mL) red seedless grapes, cut in half
> 1/2 cup (125 mL) green seedless grapes, cut in half
> 1/2 cup (125 mL) drained crushed pineapple (reserve 1 tbsp/15 mL juice)
> 1 pint (500 mL) low-fat vanilla frozen yogurt or 1% ice cream

Place the coconut in a single layer on a non-stick baking sheet and toast in a 350°F (180°C) oven for about 5 minutes. Keep an eye on the pan, as coconut burns quickly. Let cool.

Chop the orange segments coarsely and place them in a bowl. Add the grapes and pineapple with reserved juice.

Using 4 parfait glasses, place a small amount of the fruit mixture in the bottom of each glass. Divide half the yogurt among the glasses, layering it over the fruit. Add another layer of fruit, the remaining yogurt and finish with a top layer of fruit. Sprinkle the toasted coconut on the top.

Chapter 3

Bunch of Brunch Spread

Menu

Drunken Fruit
Blueberry Muffins
Sticky Fingers Bread
Rainbow Pepper Frittata
Sharp and Sweet Salad
Big Chill Poached Salmon
Old-Fashioned Ham
Mustard Sauce for Ham
Jump-Up Chutney
Saintly Scalloped Potatoes
Florentine Stuffed Shells
Twisted French Toast
Twisted French Toast Gets Sauced
Peachy Cobbler
Mocha Madness Chocolate Cake

Introduction

Brunch just seems to go with spring, although the idea of having a bunch of friends and family over for a lazy Sunday afternoon is always a good one, no matter what the season.

When we think of brunch, we think of occasions. Mother's Day. Showers. Graduation. Baskets of flowers and crisp table linens. Our version is different from the belly-busting buffets that seem to be so popular when people go out for brunch today. You know the kind — you need a forklift to get the plates back to the table, and a crane to hoist you out the door so you can go home and have a nap. And people wonder why they can't get their pants done up.

We see things differently for the Bunch of Brunch Spread. Lots of great food, sure, but we look at brunch as a way to liven up a quiet Sunday with fun company and healthy yet hearty eats. While most people are grumbling about heading back to work Monday, you can be tucking into Sticky Fingers Bread and Florentine Ricotta Shells while sipping one of our pal Hoss's classic Morning After cocktails. In Wendy and Barb land, party day is Sunday. Well, it helps if you've got Monday off!

So make Sunday Funday and get the gang together for some fabulous eats. Like the song says, Sunday will never be the same.

 Cocktails

Savory, spicy drinks just naturally go with brunch, we think. And that's especially true if one of your guests had a bit too much Saturday night going on before Sunday morning! You may also want to serve a mix of sparkling water and exotic fruit juices, or flavored ice teas along with these two brunch cocktail faves.

Bloody Tini

> **fresh cracked pepper**
> **lime wedge**
> **2 oz (50 mL) vodka**
> **2 oz (50 mL) tomato juice**
> **lime twist for garnish**

Fill a chilled glass with ice and grind pepper over top. Squeeze lime wedge over the ice. In a shaker, mix vodka and tomato juice over ice. Pour over ice in glass and garnish with lime.

Hoss's Morning After

Yes, we do know somebody named Hoss. And this is his guaranteed "cure" for what's hurtin' after a long day riding on the Ponderosa.

fresh cracked pepper
1/2 tsp (2 mL) horseradish
2 oz (50 mL) vodka
6 oz (175 mL) Clamato juice
3 drops Worcestershire sauce
lime juice
lime twist for garnish

Chill a 16-ounce (500 mL) glass in the freezer. Fill it with ice and grind pepper over. In shaker, mix the remaining ingredients. Pour into glass and garnish with lime.

Wine Suggestions
German whites
such as Liebfraumilch
(literally, mother's milk),
Riesling or Spätlese

Music Picks

 From Wendy

Andreas Vollenweider, *The Trilogy*. Columbia.

From Barb

Harry Belafonte, *Jump up Calypso*. RCA.

Serves 8

Per serving:

Calories: 141

Fat: 1 g

Drunken Fruit

Marsala is an intensely flavored sweet wine, so you don't need much to make a big impression. This salad looks lovely in a cut crystal bowl, and we often try different fruit combos, depending on what's in season and what looks good at the store.

> 1/4 cup (50 mL) peach jam
> 1/4 cup (50 mL) Marsala
> 2 pears, cored and cut in eighths
> 2 apples, cored and cut in eighths
> 2 oranges, peeled and segmented
> 2 grapefruits, peeled and segmented
> 1 honeydew melon or cantaloupe, seeded and cut
>   in chunks, or use melon baller
> 1/2 cup (125 mL) green seedless grapes
> 1/2 cup (125 mL) red seedless grapes

In a bowl, whisk together the jam and Marsala. Put all the fruit in a large serving bowl along with any reserved juice from preparation. Pour the sauce over fruit and toss gently to combine flavors. Refrigerate until ready to serve.

The Skinny on Your Waist

Looking for a quick way to tell whether you need to lose weight? Scientists at the University of Glasgow found women with waists in excess of 34 inches (86 cm) and men whose waist measurements topped 40 inches (100 cm) were generally found to be obese.

Blueberry Muffins

Makes 12

Per muffin:

Calories: 144
Fat: 3 g

We all know that those innocent muffins can be high-fat monsters. Here's a healthy version that rivals the bad-for-you kind in moist, rich blueberry taste.

> 2 cups (500 mL) all-purpose flour
> 3/4 cup (175 mL) granulated sugar
> 1 tsp (5 mL) baking powder
> 1/2 tsp (2 mL) baking soda
> 1/2 tsp (2 mL) salt
> 2 egg whites
> 1/2 cup (125 mL) low-fat lemon yogurt
> 1/2 cup (125 mL) applesauce
> 2 tbsp (30 mL) canola oil
> 1 tsp (5 mL) grated lemon zest
> 1 cup (250 mL) blueberries, fresh is best

Preheat oven to 400°F (200°C).

Combine the flour, sugar, baking powder, soda and salt in a large bowl. Combine the egg whites, yogurt, applesauce, oil and lemon zest in a second bowl. Pour wet mixture into dry ingredients and mix until just combined. Do not overmix, or muffins will be tough. Fold in blueberries. Pour batter into 12 muffin cups sprayed lightly with cooking spray.

Bake for 25 to 30 minutes. Remove to a rack and cool.

Sticky Fingers Bread

Tastes just like yummy cinnamon buns without adding pounds to yours. Mick Jagger probably can't resist this rich and gooey treat. And we can't resist Mick, so we're even.

2 1-lb (500 g) loaves frozen white bread dough
1 1/4 cups (300 mL) granulated sugar
1/4 cup (50 mL) packed brown sugar
1/4 cup (50 mL) skim milk
1 tbsp (15 mL) soft margarine
1 3/4 tsp (9 mL) cinnamon

Thaw bread dough in refrigerator overnight.

Combine 1 cup (250 mL) of the sugar, brown sugar, milk, margarine and 1 1/4 teaspoons (6 mL) cinnamon in a small saucepan. Bring to a boil and cook for 1 minute. Remove from heat and let cool for 10 minutes.

Put 1/4 cup (50 mL) sugar and 1/2 teaspoon (2 mL) cinnamon in a shallow dish and stir to combine.

Cut each loaf into 24 equal portions. Roll each portion in the sugar mixture, then layer balls of dough in a 12-cup (3L) Bundt pan or tube pan coated with cooking spray. Pour the cooled sugar syrup over the dough. Cover and let rise in a warm place for about 30 to 45 minutes, until doubled in bulk.

Preheat oven to 350°F (180°C).

Uncover dough and bake for 25 to 35 minutes until nicely browned. Remove from oven and run a knife around the edge of the pan to loosen. Invert onto a plate and remove Bundt pan. Drizzle any leftover syrup over the top.

Rainbow Pepper Frittata

Serves 4

Per serving:

Calories: 208
Fat: 5g

Kind of like an omelette, a frittata is easy to make and delicious. Once you've got the technique down, experiment with other low-fat combos, like lean meats, seafood, fat-free cheeses, veggies and herbs.

> 1 tsp (5 mL) olive oil
> 1 each of red, yellow and green peppers, diced
> 1 red onion, chopped
> 1 yellow onion, chopped
> 2 eggs
> 6 egg whites
> 1/2 tsp (2 mL) each dried basil and oregano
> salt and pepper to taste
> 1 10-oz (300 g) package frozen broccoli
> 2 tbsp (30 mL) chopped fresh parsley

In a non-stick skillet, heat the oil. Add all the peppers and onions and sauté over medium-high heat for about 10 minutes until soft but not brown.

In a large bowl, beat together the eggs and egg whites, basil, oregano, salt and pepper.

Add the frozen broccoli to the pepper mixture and stir to combine and thaw. Pour the egg mixture over the pepper mixture and lower the heat to medium. Cover and cook for about 8 minutes or just until eggs are set but still moist. Remove from heat and garnish the top of the frittata with the parsley.

The Skinny on Eggs

It's no joke, the fat's in the yolk. Using egg whites keeps volume up and fat down.

Sharp and Sweet Salad

This light, fresh salad gets its kick from the combined flavors of oranges and balsamic vinegar, that unique Italian staple made from fine wine aged in wooden casks.

2 tsp (10 mL) olive oil
2 tbsp (30 mL) balsamic vinegar
1 tbsp (15 mL) vegetable broth
1 tbsp (15 mL) honey mustard
4 cups (1 L) mixed greens
2 medium oranges, peeled and segmented

In a container with a tight-fitting lid, combine the oil, vinegar, broth and mustard. Shake well to mix.

Put the greens and oranges in a large bowl. Pour dressing over and toss gently.

The Skinny on the Salad Bar

Making a trip to the salad bar is a great way to enjoy a restaurant meal. But beware the lurking bad guys. Here are a few good and not-so-good choices. See how a couple of bad selections can make your salad about as healthy as a cheeseburger.

2 tbsp (30 mL) croutons: 60 calories, 3 g fat
2 tbsp (30 mL) shredded cheese: 56 calories, 5 g fat
2 tbsp (30 mL) chopped egg: 27 calories, 2 g fat
4 olives: 20 calories, 2 g fat
1 tbsp (15 mL) sunflower seeds: 82 calories, 7 g fat
1/4 cup (60 mL) beets: 36 calories, 0 g fat
2 tbsp (30 mL) chickpeas: 21 calories, 0 g fat
1/2 cup (125 mL) sliced mushrooms: 8 calories, 0 g fat

And remember the dressing. A quarter cup (60 mL) of regular Italian weighs in at about 300 calories with more than 30 grams of fat! Try a squeeze of lemon instead.

Big Chill Poached Salmon

This looks very impressive on any buffet table, and we're always interested in something that's this easy to make and looks (and tastes) so all-out fancy.

> 1 lemon, cut in slices
> 2 bay leaves
> 1 tbsp (15 mL) peppercorns
> 4 salmon steaks (approximately 5 oz/
>   140 g each)
> 1 cup (250 mL) non-fat sour cream
> 2 tsp (10 mL) horseradish
> 1 tbsp (15 mL) chopped fresh dill

Fill a large skillet with 3 inches (7 cm) of water. Add lemon slices, bay leaves and peppercorns and bring to a boil. Gently lower the salmon steaks into poaching liquid and reduce heat to a simmer, making sure the liquid covers steaks. Cook the salmon, uncovered, until flesh flakes easily with a fork, about 10 minutes per inch (2 cm), measuring steaks at thickest part. Remove steaks from poaching liquid. Cover them and refrigerate until serving time.

For the sauce, combine sour cream, horseradish and dill, adding a little water or skim milk if sauce is too thick. Mix well. Place salmon on a serving plate and pour a little sauce over each steak. Garnish with whole dill sprigs.

The Skinny on Fish

When it comes to whipping up a quick meal, you can't do better than fish and shellfish. In fact, most varieties take less than 10 minutes to cook — a lot faster than chicken. A rule of thumb: cook your fish for 10 minutes per inch (2.5 cm) of thickness, measuring at the thickest part. Remember not to overcook, so give it a poke to see if fish flakes easily once you get close to that 10-minute mark.

Serves 23

Per serving (3 oz/90g):

Calories: 126
Fat: 4.2 g

Old-Fashioned Ham

Somehow, people think they have to give up traditional favorites when they're modifying their diet. We say, "No way." Here's a dish that will take you and your guests back to Sunday and Grandma's with the first bite. And don't forget the mustard sauce on the side. The recipe's up next.

> 6 1/2 to 7 lb (3 kg) low-sodium, fully cooked
>   ham
> 40 whole cloves
> 1/4 cup (50 mL) packed brown sugar
> 1/4 cup (50 mL) honey
> 1/4 cup (50 mL) unsweetened pineapple juice
> 1/2 tsp (2 mL) dry mustard

Preheat oven to 425°F (220°C)

Trim fat from the ham. Score outside of the ham with a sharp knife, making a diamond-type pattern. Stud with the cloves.

Place the ham on a rack coated with cooking spray. Set the rack in a roasting pan.

Combine the sugar, honey, pineapple juice and dry mustard in a small saucepan and stir to combine. Bring to a boil and cook for 1 minute. Remove from heat and let cool. Brush sugar mixture over ham.

Bake ham for 5 minutes. Reduce heat to 325°F (160°C) and bake for another hour, basting ham every 15 minutes with sugar mixture. Remove ham from oven and let stand 10 minutes before carving.

Mustard Sauce
for Ham

Makes about
¾ cup (180 mL)

Per serving
(2 tbsp/30 ml):

Calories: 40
Fat: 1.1 g

1/4 cup (50 mL) Dijon mustard
1 tsp (5 mL) dry mustard
1/4 cup (50 mL) granulated sugar
2 tbsp (30 mL) white vinegar
1 tbsp (15 mL) canola oil
1 small bunch fresh dill, finely chopped

Combine the Dijon mustard, dry mustard, sugar, vinegar and oil
in a blender and blend until mixture comes together. Stir in the
dill and refrigerate until ready to use.

**Makes 2 cups
(500 mL)**

**Per serving
(1 oz/25 g):**

**Calories: 14
Fat: 0.1 g**

Jump-Up Chutney

We named this chutney Jump-Up for its Caribbean influence. Little bit sweet, little bit spicy. Kind of like us! Not only does it go well with the ham, it's also delicious with grilled fish or chicken. Spread a little on a turkey sandwich. It's terrific.

> 3 large mangoes, peeled and coarsely chopped
> 1/2 cup (125 mL) apple juice
> 1/2 cup (125 mL) apple cider vinegar
> 1/2 cup (125 mL) packed brown sugar
> 1 sweet onion, finely chopped
> 2 tsp (10 mL) freshly grated ginger
> 1 jalapeño pepper, seeded and minced
> 1/4 tsp (1 mL) ground cardamom
> 1/2 tsp (2 mL) cinnamon

Combine all ingredients in a small non-aluminum saucepan and bring to a boil. Reduce heat and simmer for about 45 minutes, uncovered, stirring occasionally until sauce thickens. Remove from heat and let cool. Put in a container with a tightly fitting lid and refrigerate until ready to use.

Saintly Scalloped Potatoes

Serves 4

Per serving:

Calories: 204
Fat: 3.2 g

What's a ham without scalloped potatoes sharing the plate? We dropped the cream and zipper-busting cheese to create our version of these home-style favorites.

> 1 tsp (5 mL) soft margarine
> 1 cup (250 mL) thinly sliced onions
> 1/4 tsp (1 mL) dried thyme
> 1 1/2 cups (375 mL) evaporated skim milk
> 1 1/2 tbsp (25 mL) all-purpose flour
> 1/8 tsp (0.5 mL) nutmeg
> salt and pepper to taste
> 4 cups (1 L) potatoes, peeled and thinly sliced

Preheat oven to 400°F (200°C).

In a large non-stick skillet, melt the margarine. Add the onions and thyme and sauté over medium heat for about 5 minutes.

In a bowl, stir together the evaporated milk, flour, nutmeg, salt and pepper. Use a wire whisk to make sure the mixture is smooth and lump-free. Spray a casserole dish with cooking spray. Put the sautéed onions and the potatoes in the bottom of the dish and pour the milk mixture over. Cover and bake for about 35 minutes. Lower the heat to 350°F (180°C) and bake an additional 30 minutes or until potatoes are tender.

Serve immediately.

Serves 8
Per serving:

Calories: 208
Fat: 5 g

Florentine Stuffed Shells

Spinach and creamy ricotta cheese go together so well, we thought they'd be a natural choice to play the role of "comfort food" on our brunch buffet spread. Dig in.

> 1 12-oz (375 g) box large pasta shells
>   (30 to 35 shells)
> 3 1/4 cups (8100 mL) low-fat ricotta
> 1 cup (250 mL) chopped cooked spinach,
>   fresh or frozen
> 2 green onions, chopped
> 2 tbsp (30 mL) chopped fresh parsley
> 1/4 cup (50 mL) skim milk
> 1/4 cup (50 mL) Parmesan cheese
> 2 cups (500 mL) tomato sauce,
>   fresh or jarred

Cook pasta shells according to package directions. Drain and set aside.

Preheat oven to 350° F (175° C).

In a large bowl, combine ricotta, spinach, green onions, parsley, milk and 1 tablespoon (15 mL) Parmesan.

Place shells in a baking dish and put some of the stuffing mixture in each shell.

Pour the tomato sauce over top and sprinkle with the remaining Parmesan. Bake for about 20 minutes or until hot and bubbly.

Twisted French Toast

Serves 4

**Per serving
(2 slices):**

**Calories: 382
Fat: 3.8 g**

The first twist is you "marinate" the French Toast overnight and that makes it cook up puffy and light. The second twist is this is guilt-free French Toast. Omit the butter and syrup and try our special sauce instead. The recipe follows.

> 1 egg
> 2 egg whites
> 3/4 cup (175 mL) skim milk
> 2 tbsp (30 mL) granulated sugar
> 1 tsp (5 mL) vanilla
> 1/4 tsp (1 mL) cinnamon
> 1/8 tsp (0.5 mL) baking powder
> 8 1/2-inch (1 cm) thick slices Italian bread
> 2 tsp (10 mL) soft margarine

In a large bowl, whisk together the egg, egg whites, milk, sugar, vanilla, cinnamon and baking powder.

Place bread slices in the bottom of a large, shallow dish and pour the egg mixture over the bread, turning the slices to make sure they're well-coated. Cover the dish with plastic wrap and refrigerate overnight.

To cook French Toast: Heat 1 teaspoon (5 mL) margarine in a non-stick skillet. Add as many bread slices to the pan as will fit and cook about 3 minutes per side until golden brown. Repeat with remaining bread slices, adding remaining margarine if needed.

Twisted French Toast Gets Sauced

That Granny Smith. A bit tart, but that's why we love her.

1 cup (250 mL) apple juice
4 Granny Smith apples, peeled, cored and diced
1 tsp (5 mL) lemon juice
1 tsp (5 mL) grated lemon zest
pinch of pumpkin pie spice
2/3 cup (150 mL) raisins

In a medium saucepan, cook the apple juice, apples, lemon juice, lemon zest and pumpkin pie spice over medium heat for 10 minutes. Transfer to a food processor or blender and blend to a chunky purée. Return sauce to the pan and stir in the raisins. Keep warm until ready to serve.

Peachy Cobbler

Serves 6

Per serving:

Calories: 173
Fat: 4 g

Always good, this stuff is unbelievable when summer peaches are at their super-sweet peak.

> 4 cups (1 L) sliced peaches (fresh or canned,
>   unsweetened and drained)
> 2 tbsp (30 mL) lemon juice
> 1/2 cup (125 mL) whole wheat flour
> 1/3 cup (75 mL) brown sugar
> 1 tsp (5 mL) cinnamon
> 2 tbsp (30 mL) margarine

Preheat oven to 375°F (190°C).

Place the peaches in a shallow casserole dish and sprinkle with lemon juice.

In a bowl, combine the flour, sugar and cinnamon. Cut in the margarine with a pastry blender or a fork until the mixture is crumbly. Spread mixture over peaches. Bake for about 30 minutes.

Serve with 1% low-fat ice cream or low-fat frozen vanilla yogurt.

Serves 16

Per serving:

Calories: 222
Fat: 4 g

Mocha Madness Chocolate Cake

You know we love chocolate, especially Barb, our Countess Chocula. Can't have a brunch without chocolate, we always say. Can't do anything without chocolate, come to think of it.

1 3/4 cups (425 mL) all-purpose flour
1 cup (250 mL) granulated sugar
1 cup (250 mL) packed brown sugar
3/4 cup (175 mL) unsweetened cocoa powder
1 1/2 tsp (7 mL) baking soda
1 1/2 tsp (7 mL) baking powder
1 tsp (5 mL) salt
1 1/4 cups (300 mL) buttermilk
2 eggs, lightly beaten
1/4 cup (50 mL) canola oil
2 tsp (10 mL) vanilla
1 cup (250 mL) hot, strong, black coffee

Icing:
1 cup (250 mL) confectioner's sugar
1/2 tsp (2 mL) vanilla
1 to 2 tbsp (15 to 30 mL) buttermilk or skim milk

Preheat oven to 350°F (180°C).

Spray a 12-cup (3 L) Bundt pan or tube pan with cooking spray. Dust pan with some flour and shake out the excess.

In a large bowl, whisk together the flour, sugar, cocoa, baking soda, powder and salt. Add the buttermilk, brown sugar, eggs, oil and vanilla. Beat with an electric mixer on high for 2 minutes. Whisk in hot coffee.

Pour batter into the pan and bake for 45 to 50 minutes until tester comes out clean. Cool cake in the pan, then invert onto a wire rack to cool completely.

Icing: In a bowl, whisk sugar, vanilla and enough of the milk to make a thick icing but thin enough to drizzle on the cake and have it run down the sides.

The Skinny on Labels

"Read the label," everybody says. But what if you can't make heads or tails of it anyway? If you see these words on the label, here's what's inside:

Fat free: Not completely no fat, but less than 1/2 gram per serving.

Calorie free: Again, not free. It means fewer than 5 calories per serving.

Low fat: Fewer than 3 grams of fat per serving.

Light or Lite: The product must have one-third fewer calories, or 50% less calories than the regular version. If 50% of the original calories came from fat, then fat has to be chopped by 50% or more. Yes, it's confusing, so check out the nutrition panel on the package.

Reduced fat: It all depends on how fatty the original product is. It only has to be 25% lower in fat, which is why reduced fat chips can still pack a high-calorie wallop.

Chapter 4

Everything but the Ants Picnic Spread

Menu

Wacky Teriyaki Salad

This Ain t the Waldorf Slaw

Tuna-rific Pasta Salad

Santa Fe Veggie Roll-Ups

Curry Some Flavor Turkey Pitas

Scarlett Never Had It So Good Southern Unfried Chicken

Pucker-Up Pickles

Mum s Chutney

Magnificent Meatloaf for Sandwiches

Fruit Kebobs with Two Dipping Sauces

Blueberry Betty

Introduction

Apicnic is like a mini-holiday, an afternoon in a sun-splashed park, along a shaded riverbank, or crowded around a backyard picnic table, chomping on sweet watermelon so ripe the juice runs down your arm.

No matter how you approach picnics, whether it's Barb-style with her hubby and son, a basket filled with goodies for a day at the park with a few other couples who have kids the same age, or your taste is more like Wendy's, a romantic hamper and a lazy afternoon for two, picnics can't be beat.

Picnic food has to be portable, something that fits into a cooler or basket. But there's more to it than the old sandwich and tub of fatty potato salad routine. We wanted to experiment, bringing out food so delicious and interesting, nobody has to be called twice for lunch. And you'll be up for a spirited Frisbee toss when you finish. Santa Fe Veggie Roll-Ups are easy to eat and taste terrific. Our Wacky Teriyaki Salad and Tuna-rific Pasta Salad combine low fat with fabulous taste. And Scarlett Never Had It So Good Unfried Chicken will ring your southern belle, sugar.

You probably have picnic memories of your own. Maybe it's the lake you stumbled on one day while exploring for a spot, or the old, red-checked blanket that you always sat on as a kid. Perhaps it's as simple as the smell of a wicker basket or fresh-mowed grass, or the delightful freedom you had as a kid to plonk yourself down, eat with your hands, get messy, not care, and wash off by splashing in the lake or river beside your picnic site.

It's that freedom we wanted to bring to the Everything but the Ants Picnic Spread. It's the freedom to eat fantastic food and still look great in shorts, to be able to nibble and munch and never feel guilty. To make that mess and eat with your hands. Be a kid again. Go ahead and dive in the lake if you get covered in food. But hurry back, there's a lot still to eat. And even though we didn't invite the ants, they sometimes show up anyway.

Sip Picks

We can't imagine a picnic without lemonade served from one of those giant cooler dispensers, the ice rattling inside as you tip it to pour the frosty drink on a hot day. This recipe is so good, you might want to quit your job and open a stand. It's perfect for all ages. If the big folks are so inclined, vodka or gin will turn it into a refreshing cocktail.

Homemade Lemonade

> 1/2 cup (125 mL) water
> 1 1/2 cups (375 mL) granulated sugar
> juice of 5 lemons
> 3 cups (750 mL) 7-Up
> 2 1/2 cups (625 mL) club soda

For simple syrup, mix water and sugar in a saucepan and heat until sugar melts. Cool before using.

Mix cooled syrup with remaining ingredients in a large container and refrigerate until ready to serve. Pour into tall, ice-filled glasses and garnish with lime slices or mint.

Music Picks

From Wendy
Steely Dan, *The Best of Steely Dan*. MCA.

From Barb
Chicago, *Overtime*. Astral.

Wacky Teriyaki Salad

Serves 6

Per serving:

Calories: 50
Fat: 0.6 g

Teriyaki sauce gives this colorful salad its kick. It will make you give up the boring old standby of bottled diet Italian dressing on mixed veggie salad for good.

    1 cup (250 mL) broccoli florets
    2 large carrots, cut in thin julienne strips
    1/2 head red cabbage, sliced thinly
    1 1/2 cups (375 mL) cucumber, cut in julienne
    1/2 cup (125 mL) red pepper, cut in julienne
    1 tbsp (15 mL) rice vinegar
    1 tbsp (15 mL) low-sodium teriyaki sauce
    1 tsp (5 mL) granulated sugar
    1/4 tsp (1 mL) chili oil

Combine all the vegetables in a large bowl.

Mix together vinegar, teriyaki sauce, sugar and oil. Pour dressing over vegetables and toss gently.

Cover and refrigerate 2 hours to let flavors blend.

The Skinny on Oriental Ingredients

These should be easy to find in most grocery stores. If not, check out markets in your local Chinatown, if you're lucky enough to have one. Most sauces and condiments are low in fat, and the oils are bursting with intense flavor, so a little goes a long way. Some sauces are high in sugar, though, so check labels.

Serves 8

Per serving:

Calories: 92
Fat: 2 g

This Ain't the Waldorf Slaw

This is a bit of Waldorf salad and a bit of carrot slaw mixed together in a low-fat yogurt base. Keep it in the cooler when you picnic.

    2 medium apples, diced
    1 1/2 cups (375 mL) grated carrots
    1/3 cup (75 mL) raisins
    1/4 cup (50 mL) chopped walnuts
    1/2 cup (125 mL) plain non-fat yogurt
    2 tbsp (30 mL) honey

In a large bowl, combine the apples, carrots, raisins and walnuts.
    Whisk together the yogurt and honey until combined.
    Pour the dressing over the carrot-apple mixture and toss gently until combined.
    Cover and refrigerate until ready to serve.

Tuna-rific Pasta Salad

Serves 8

Per serving:

Calories: 217
Fat: 3 g

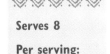

Tuna pasta salad is so good, we couldn't leave it out of our picnic spread. But we left the fat and calories at home with the ants. We promise you won't miss either of them.

    1 8-oz (250 g) package small pasta shells
    1 10-oz (300 g) package frozen peas
    2 6.8-oz cans (170 g) water-packed tuna
    2 green onions, minced
    2 tbsp (30 mL) low-fat mayonnaise
    3/4 cup (175 mL) plain non-fat yogurt
    1 tbsp (15 mL) Dijon mustard
    1 clove garlic, minced
    salt and pepper to taste

Cook pasta shells according to package directions. Drain and set aside.

In a small saucepan, cook the peas according to package directions. Drain and set aside.

In a large bowl, combine tuna, green onions, mayonnaise, yogurt, mustard, garlic, salt and pepper. Mix lightly. Add the cooked pasta and peas and toss all ingredients together.

Cover and refrigerate until serving time.

Santa Fe Veggie Roll-Ups

These Tex-Mex inspired roll-ups are a hit with everybody. Crunchy, packed with a bunch of neat flavors, they also make a great packed lunch for adults and kids.

> 1/2 cup (125 mL) Yogo cheese (see page 14 for recipe) or low-fat cream cheese
> 1 green onion, chopped
> 1 tbsp (15 mL) chopped fresh coriander
> 1 tbsp (15 mL) lime juice
> 1 tsp (5 mL) olive oil
> 1/8 tsp (0.5 mL) cumin
> 1/8 tsp (0.5 mL) salt
> 1 large green pepper, sliced
> 1 large yellow pepper, sliced
> 4 8-inch flour tortillas
> 4 lettuce leaves

Combine Yogo and green onion.

In a large bowl, combine the coriander, lime juice, oil, cumin and salt. Add the peppers and toss to coat.

Spread out 1 tortilla and top with 2 tablespoons (30 mL) of the Yogo mixture, spreading almost to edge of tortilla.

Top with 1 lettuce leaf, then one-quarter of the pepper mixture. Roll up tightly and wrap with plastic wrap. Repeat procedure with remaining tortillas and refrigerate until ready to serve.

At serving time, cut roll-ups in half diagonally, or let the kids peel the wrap back and eat like a banana.

Curry Some Flavor Turkey Pitas

Serves 4

Per serving:

Calories: 279
Fat: 7 g

These pitas are a change from standard turkey sandwiches, and the bits of apple add a hint of sweetness. A great way to use left-over turkey or chicken, too.

> 1/4 cup (50 mL) low-fat mayonnaise
> 1/4 cup (50 mL) plain non-fat yogurt
> 3/4 tsp (5 mL) curry powder
> 1/8 tsp (0.5 mL) salt
> 1/8 tsp (0.5 mL) red pepper flakes
> 1 clove garlic, minced
> 2 cups (500 mL) diced cooked turkey
> 4 green onions, chopped
> 1 large red pepper, seeded and chopped
> 1 small apple, cored and diced
> 2 tbsp (30 mL) chopped fresh parsley
> 4 lettuce leaves
> 4 whole wheat pitas

In a large bowl, whisk together the mayonnaise, yogurt, curry, salt, pepper flakes and garlic.

Stir in the cooked turkey, green onions, red pepper, apple and parsley. Mix well to combine all of the ingredients.

Cut lettuce leaves and pitas in half. Place one half lettuce leaf in one pita half and stuff with about one-eighth of the turkey mixture. Repeat with remaining pita halves. Wrap each half in plastic wrap and refrigerate until ready to serve.

Scarlett Never Had It So Good Southern Unfried Chicken

Now, sugar, you don't think us li'l ol' Burlington belles were about to send you off on a picnic without some southern fried, did you? You're right. We're not. We go one better with our "unfried" version of the picnic classic that might just put a certain Colonel out of business.

> 1 cup (250 mL) cornmeal
> 1/4 tsp (1 mL) black pepper
> 2 tbsp (30 mL) chopped fresh parsley
> 4 boneless, skinless chicken breasts
> 1/3 cup (75 mL) Dijon mustard

Preheat oven and baking sheet to 450°F (230°C).

In a large plastic bag, combine cornmeal, pepper and parsley.

Brush each chicken breast all over with a little of the Dijon mustard and put the breasts, one at a time, in the bag with the cornmeal mixture. Put on some funky tunes and shake, shake, shake to coat evenly.

Repeat procedure with remaining chicken breasts.

Place coated chicken breasts on a rack sprayed with cooking spray set on top of the pre-heated cookie sheet.

Bake for 30 to 35 minutes. Serve warm or cold.

The Skinny on Quick Tips to Cut Fat in the Kitchen

1. Use a roasting pan to drain fat when cooking meats and poultry.
2. Substitute non-fat yogurt or non-fat sour cream for mayonnaise and full-fat sour cream.
3. Thicken soups and sauces with all-purpose flour and water mixed to a thin paste instead of adding cream.
4. Marinate for flavor. You won't miss the fat.
5. Use a non-stick frying pan and cooking spray for all sautéeing.
6. Roast, broil or grill instead of frying.

**Makes 7 cups
(1.75 L)**

**Per serving
(¼ cup/60 mL):**

**Calories: 23
Fat: 0.1 g**

Pucker-Up Pickles

Can't have a picnic without pickles, and these are winners. Make you pucker, but sweet as a kiss.

> **6 cups (1.5 L) thinly sliced cucumbers**
> **2 cups (500 mL) thinly sliced onions**
> **1 1/2 cups (375 mL) white vinegar**
> **1 cup (250 mL) granulated sugar**
> **1/2 tsp (2 mL) salt**
> **1/2 tsp (2 mL) mustard seed**
> **1/2 tsp (2 mL) celery seed**
> **1/2 tsp (2 mL) ground turmeric**

Put half the cucumbers in a large bowl and top with half the onions. Repeat the layers with the remaining cucumbers and onions.

Combine the vinegar, sugar, salt, mustard seed, celery seed and turmeric in a saucepan. Whisk to combine all ingredients and bring to a boil. Cook for 1 minute.

Pour the vinegar mixture over the cucumbers and onions and marinate, covered, in the refrigerator for 4 days. These pickles will keep in the refrigerator for up to 1 month.

Mum's Chutney

Everybody loves Wendy's mum, who also happens to be a great cook. We think this chutney is a delectable addition to our picnic spread. Try it on our meatloaf sandwiches. That's the next recipe.

> 3 tomatoes, chopped
> 3 peaches, chopped
> 3 pears, chopped
> 2 green onions, chopped
> 1 onion, chopped
> 2 1/2 cups (675 mL) granulated sugar
> 1 cup (250 mL) white wine vinegar
> 1/2 tsp (2 mL) salt
> 1/2 tbsp (7 mL) pickling spice, wrapped and tied
>   in a piece of cheesecloth

Place all ingredients in a large saucepan. Bring to a boil and lower heat to medium.

Simmer for 1 1/2 hours. Discard pickling spice. Refrigerate until serving time.

Serves 8

Per serving:

Calories: 90
Fat: 2.9 g

Magnificent Meatloaf for Sandwiches

2 lb (1 kg) ground turkey
1 onion, finely chopped
1 egg white
1/2 cup (125 mL) bread crumbs
1/2 cup (125 mL) chopped fresh parsley
1 tsp (5 mL) dried oregano
salt and pepper to taste

Preheat oven to 350°F (180°C).

In a large bowl, combine all ingredients and mix well. Pack the meat mixture into a loaf pan and bake for 50 to 60 minutes.

Remove loaf from oven and let cool. Refrigerate meatloaf in the loaf pan so when it's time to pack for the picnic, it will be easily transportable. When ready to serve, slice loaf and serve on fresh whole wheat bread, in a pita or in your favorite type of bread. Garnish with Mum's Chutney, if you like.

Fruit Kebobs with Two Dipping Sauces

Serves 6
Per serving:

Calories: 120
Fat: 0 g

Kids just love these skewers of sweet summer fruit. Must have something to do with the dipping sauce. Big people love 'em, too.

>   1/2 large pineapple, halved, cored and cut in
>   triangles 1/2-inch (1 cm) thick
>   2 cups (500 mL) fresh strawberries, washed and
>   hulled
>   5 kiwis, peeled and sliced 1/2-inch (1 cm) thick
>   1 cup (250 mL) large grapes, seedless green, red,
>   or a combination
>   4 large oranges cut in half, each half cut in 3
>   wedges
>   8 bamboo skewers
>   juice of 1 lemon

Thread the pieces of fruit alternately on the skewers. Place in a shallow baking or serving dish and squeeze the lemon juice over each skewer. Refrigerate until ready to serve. Serve with the following dipping sauces.

Makes 1½ cups
(375 mL)

Per serving
(2 tbsp/30 mL):

Calories: 34
Fat: 0 g

Dipping Sauces for Fruit Kebobs

Raspberry-Poppyseed Dip

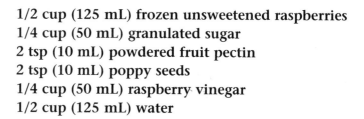

1/2 cup (125 mL) frozen unsweetened raspberries
1/4 cup (50 mL) granulated sugar
2 tsp (10 mL) powdered fruit pectin
2 tsp (10 mL) poppy seeds
1/4 cup (50 mL) raspberry vinegar
1/2 cup (125 mL) water

In a blender, combine all the ingredients and blend until smooth. Store in the refrigerator until ready to serve. Place in an attractive bowl and serve alongside the fruit kebobs.

Clockwise from top:
Wacky Teriyaki Salad (p. 77)
Fruit Kebobs with Dipping Sauces (p. 87)
Santa Fe Veggie Roll-Ups (p. 80)
Curry Some Flavor Turkey Pitas (p. 81)
This Ain't the Waldorf Slaw (p. 78)
Scarlett Never Had It So Good Southern Unfried Chicken (p. 82)

Sweet and Creamy Dip

Makes 1¼ cups
(300 mL)

Per serving
(2 tbsp/30 mL):

Calories: 7
Fat: 0 g

1 cup (250 mL) non-fat sour cream
2 tbsp (30 mL) brown sugar
2 tbsp (30 mL) skim milk

Combine sour cream and sugar in a bowl and stir until thoroughly combined. Add the milk a little at a time to make a smooth consistency.

Refrigerate until ready to serve. Serve alongside fruit kebobs for dipping. The slightly tart taste of the sour cream goes very well with the fruit.

Clockwise from top:
Splish Splash Lemon Ice (p. 108)
Dive-In Pita Chips (p. 95)
We Be Jammin' Onion Jam (p. 96)
Rainbow Pepper Relish (p. 107)
Tiki Torch Chicken Satays (p. 98)
Polynesian Sweet Garlic Sauce (p. 99)
Bayou B.B.Q. Shrimp (p. 97)
Grill 'Em Danno Grilled Pineapple (p. 110)
Beach Blanket Bingo Potato Salad (p. 100)
Cluck It Up Chicken Burgers (p. 105)
Cranberry Ketchup (p. 106)

Serves 8

Per serving:

Calories: 144
Fat: 1 g

Blueberry Betty

This proves once and for all why Betty is more popular than Veronica. Who ever heard of Blueberry Ronnie?

> 2 cups (500 mL) fresh or frozen, thawed blueberries
> 1/4 cup (50 mL) granulated sugar
> juice of 1 large lemon
> 4 cups (1 L) bread cubes 1/2-inch (1 cm) square, white or whole wheat
> 1/3 cup (75 mL) packed brown sugar
> 1 tsp (5 mL) ground cinnamon

Preheat oven to 350°F (180°C).

In a large bowl, combine the blueberries, sugar and lemon juice.

In a second bowl, combine the bread cubes, brown sugar and cinnamon.

In a 9-inch (22 cm) square baking pan, spread a layer of the fruit mixture, then a layer of the bread cube mixture; repeat.

Bake for about 30 minutes.

Chapter 5

Twisting by the Pool Spread

Menu

Dive-In Pita Chips
We Be Jammin Onion Jam
Bayou B.B.Q. Shrimp
Tiki Torch Chicken Satays
Polynesian Sweet Garlic Sauce
Beach Blanket Bingo Potato Salad
Lean and Luscious Cobb Salad
Annette Funicello Italian Burgers
Cluck It Up Chicken Burgers
Cranberry Ketchup
Rainbow Pepper Relish
Splish Splash Lemon Ice
Strawberry Blonde Shortcake
Grill Em Danno Grilled Pineapple

Introduction

If you can't stand the heat, get out of your kitchen and into the backyard.

No, you don't need a pool to make the delightful summer menu in this spread. We don't, and we do all the time. Actually, we're lucky enough to have a few friends with swimming pools, and we often get invited over for an afternoon dip on a sweltering Saturday, mainly because we bring the delicious, low-fat food. So take a page from our cookbook and do likewise.

You know, the idea here is not so much to cavort in the pool, but to get outdoors and enjoy informal entertaining at its best, whether it's family, friends from the office or a get-to-know-the-neighbors party. Keep it simple with paper plates and plastic glasses. Why not pick up some inexpensive paper leis at the party supply store to offer your guests as they come in? And don't forget those little paper umbrellas for the drinks.

There's something about the smell of a barbecue, the glow of coals at dusk, the light cast by patio lanterns, candles or tiki torches that seems to instantly take you back to lazy, hazy and, hopefully, very crazy summers past.

The treats in this spread are easy to make and most can be prepared ahead of time, giving you more time to hang out with your guests and enjoy yourself. These are our favorite dishes to take to a pool party or enjoy in our pool-less backyards, tried and true hits like We Be Jammin' Onion Jam, Tiki Torch Chicken Satays with Polynesian Sweet Garlic Sauce, Beach Blanket Bingo Potato Salad and luscious Strawberry Blonde Shortcake.

So fire up the grill, dust off the picnic table, put on some party music (check out our suggestions, coming up in this chapter) and have a blast. With our low-fat versions of cookout fare, you won't be worried about slipping into your swimsuit and taking the plunge. Come on in, the spread's just fine.

 Cocktails

The Sea Breeze is the ultimate "twistin' by the pool" cocktail. It's tall, cool and refreshing and your guests will think it's a blast if you serve them in colorful plastic glasses garnished with a few chunks of fruit. Won't you let us take you on a Sea Breeze cruise?

Sea Breeze

2 oz (50 mL) vodka
2 oz (50 mL) cranberry juice
3 oz (60 mL) fresh-squeezed grapefruit juice

Mix all ingredients well and pour into a tall glass over lots of ice.

Wine Suggestions
Chardonnay or Fumé Blanc

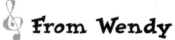

Music Picks

From Wendy

Kim Mitchell, *Shakin' Like a Human Being*. Alert.

From Barb

Various Artists, *Flamenco — Fire and Grace*. Narada/Universal.

Dive-In Pita Chips

Makes 64 chips

Per chip:

Calories: 7
Fat: trace

These chips work very well without the oil, so it's up to you whether you include it.

4 large pita breads
1 tbsp (15 mL) olive oil

Preheat oven to 350°F (180°C).

Separate each pita in half by using a sharp knife and cutting around the outside. You will have 8 thin slices. Use a pastry brush to brush the oil on each. Cut each slice into 8 wedges. Arrange the wedges in a single layer on a baking sheet and bake for 8 to 10 minutes until brown and lightly crisped.

The Skinny on Water

Your body needs water, and most of us don't drink enough. The 8-glass thing should be looked at as a guide, not a rule. But drinking water keeps your body's internal waterworks functioning efficiently and keeps your skin hydrated, making it look younger. So drink up.

**Makes 1 cup
(250 mL)**

**Per serving
(1 tbsp/15 mL):**

**Calories: 53
Fat: 0**

We Be Jammin'
Onion Jam

This flavorful jam looks so pretty on the table and makes a great dip for Dive-in Pita Chips. Or spread it on your burgers, chicken, just about any grilled food. Turn up the heat with more cayenne if you're in the mood for some "ooo, baby" in your life.

> **1 lb (500 g) red onions, peeled and
>   thinly sliced
> 1/4 cup (50 mL) balsamic vinegar
> 2 cups (500 mL) dry red wine
> 2 cups (500 mL) water
> 1/4 cup (50 mL) honey
> 2 tbsp (30 mL) granulated sugar
> pinch of cayenne pepper
> pinch of ground cloves
> salt and pepper to taste**

In a large non-aluminum saucepan, combine the onions, vinegar, wine, water, honey, sugar, cayenne and cloves. Bring the mixture to a boil and reduce heat. Simmer over low heat until most of the liquid is absorbed, about 45 minutes. Stir occasionally during the cooking process, making sure onions don't burn as liquid level goes down.

Remove from heat and cool. Taste to check seasoning and add salt and pepper to taste.

Bayou B.B.Q. Shrimp

Serves 10

Per serving:

Calories: 90
Fat: 3.6 g

There's a reason Australians think "slipping a shrimp on the barbie" is the height of hospitality. It's because they taste so darned good. Shrimp and spicy barbecue sauce go together like, well, Wendy and Barb. And the best part about this recipe is that you can make it even when it rains, getting great B.B.Q. taste straight from your stovetop.

> 1 tsp (5 mL) paprika
> 1/4 tsp (1 mL) black pepper
> 1/4 tsp (1 mL) cayenne pepper
> 1/2 tsp (2 mL) dried oregano
> 1/4 tsp (1 mL) dried thyme
> 1 1/2 lb (750 g) medium shrimp, cleaned and
>   deveined
> 1 tsp (5 mL) olive oil
> 1 onion, chopped fine
> 2 cloves garlic, chopped fine
> 1/4 cup (50 mL) Worcestershire sauce
> 1 tbsp (15 mL) lemon juice
> 1 cup (250 mL) water
> 2 tbsp (30 mL) chopped parsley

In a small bowl, combine the paprika, black pepper, cayenne, oregano and thyme. Divide spice mixture in half. Toss the shrimp with half of the spice mixture.

Heat the oil in a skillet and add onion and garlic. Sauté about 5 minutes until softened and just lightly colored. Add the remaining spice mix and cook for 1 minute. Add the Worcestershire sauce, lemon juice and water. Bring to a boil and cook uncovered until reduced to about 1/2 cup (125 mL).

Add shrimp to sauce and stir to combine. Cook for about 3 minutes until shrimp are just cooked. Place in serving dish and garnish with the parsley.

**Makes 16
skewers**

Per skewer:

**Calories: 62
Fat: 1.6 g**

Tiki Torch Chicken Satays with Polynesian Sweet Garlic Sauce

These yummy little skewers are easy to eat while you're hanging
out around the pool. The curry adds a twist to the teriyaki flavor,
and the sweet and sassy Polynesian dipping sauce completes the
South Seas flavors.

> 16 bamboo skewers soaked in cold water
>   for 30 minutes
> 1 tsp (5 mL) curry powder
> 1 clove garlic, minced
> 1 tbsp (15 mL) soy sauce
> 1 tbsp (15 mL) lemon juice
> 1 tbsp (15 mL) honey
> 1 tbsp (15 mL) water
> 1 lb (500 g) boneless skinless chicken breasts cut
>   in 4 x 1-inch (10 x 2 cm) strips

In a large bowl, combine the curry, garlic, soy sauce, lemon juice,
honey and water. Add the chicken strips and marinate in the
refrigerator for 1 hour.

Thread 1 chicken strip on each skewer and grill on medium-
high heat 4 minutes per side until chicken is cooked through.
Serve with Polynesian Sweet Garlic Sauce.

Polynesian Sweet Garlic Sauce

Makes 1¾ cups
(425 mL)

Per serving
(1½ tbsp/20 mL):

Calories: 50
Fat: 0g

Feel like a dip? C'mon in, the sauce is fine.

> 1/2 cup (125 mL) rice wine vinegar
> 1 cup (250 mL) water
> 1/2 cup (125 mL) packed brown sugar
> 3 tbsp (45 mL) finely minced garlic
> 2 tsp (10 mL) chili paste
> 1/2 tsp (2 mL) salt

Place all the ingredients in a small saucepan. Simmer, uncovered, over medium-low heat until sauce has thickened, about 30 minutes. Watch closely near the end so it doesn't burn on the bottom. Serve with chicken satays. Sauce will keep in refrigerator up to 1 week, tightly covered.

10 Best Places to Have a Party, Wendy and Barb Style

1. Art gallery or museum
2. Your kitchen
3. On a boat
4. On a beach beneath the stars
5. In your backyard with tiki torches, lanterns and a kiddie wading pool chilling the wine
6. In a limousine, blindfolded
7. In the library
8. In your office
9. At a comedy club
10. At a skating rink or hockey arena

Serves 6

Per serving:

Calories: 165

Fat 3 g

Beach Blanket Bingo
Potato Salad

We've always loved the beach party movies. Okay, Barb saw them in reruns. But those wacky kids dancing on the sand, surfer boys chowing down on picnic lunches made by loyal gal pals and the non-stop music put us in a summer party mood. And potato salad is always on the menu.

> 2 lb (1 kg) small red-skinned potatoes, scrubbed,
>   cut in 2-inch (5 cm) pieces
> 1 cup (250 mL) frozen peas
> 2 roasted red peppers, fresh or jarred, diced
> 2 tbsp (30 mL) red wine vinegar
> 2 cloves garlic, minced
> 1 tsp (5 mL) pepper
> 1/2 tsp (2 mL) salt
> 1 tbsp (15 mL) olive oil
> 1/2 cup (125 mL) plain non-fat yogurt
> 1/4 cup (50 mL) chopped fresh chives

In a large pot of boiling water, blanch the peas for 30 seconds then remove with a slotted spoon. Add the potatoes and cook 15 to 20 minutes until tender. Drain.

Put potatoes and peas in a large bowl and add the red peppers.

In another bowl, whisk together the vinegar, garlic, pepper, salt, oil and yogurt. Pour the dressing over potatoes and toss gently, being careful not to break up potatoes. Put them in a serving bowl and garnish with chives.

The Skinny on Roasted Peppers

To make your own, place red peppers on the grill or under the broiler and cook until the skins blacken. Keep turning so they char evenly. Put them in a paper bag, or in a bowl covered by a tea towel, and let cool. The skins will peel off easily. If you use jarred peppers, check the label. If they are packed in oil, make sure you rinse them well with hot water and pat dry.

Lean and Luscious Cobb Salad

Cobb Salad is a California tradition, but the classic recipe couldn't be worse for your waist, containing an ingredient list that reads like a who's who of high fat. But we love Cobb Salad, so what to do? Easy. We came up with a delectable, low-fat, Wendy and Barb version just for you that looks just as dramatic on your table.

Salad:
1 red pepper, diced
1 green pepper, diced
2 cups (500 mL) frozen peas
6 cups (1.5 L) romaine lettuce
3 oz (85 g) low-fat cheddar cheese, shredded
1 6-inch (15 cm) cucumber, thinly sliced
2 hard-cooked eggs, whites chopped and yolks
     discarded
8 green onions, thinly sliced

In a large pot of boiling water, blanch the peppers for 30 seconds. Remove them with a slotted spoon to a colander. Rinse under cold water and set aside.

Add the peas to the water and blanch for 30 seconds. Drain and rinse under cold water. Set aside.

On a large serving platter, make a bed of the romaine lettuce, which serves as a base. Arrange the remaining ingredients in rows going out from the center, like spokes on a wheel. Using half the cheese, start at one edge of the plate and, working toward the center, make a row of cheese. Next to that make a row with half the peppers. Using half the cucumber slices make a row, overlapping each slice slightly, followed by a row of half the peas. Then make a row, of half the egg whites. At the halfway point, make a line of green onions across the plate, then repeat the spokes to finish the plate. You can toss the salad ingredients with the dressing after your guests have admired your handiwork, or simply drizzle dressing over the whole salad and serve with tongs.

Dressing:
3/4 cup (175 mL) tomato or V8 juice
1/4 cup (50 mL) red wine vinegar
1 tbsp (15 mL) chopped fresh parsley
1 tbsp (15 mL) chopped green onions
1 clove garlic, crushed
1/4 tsp (1 mL) granulated sugar
3 drops Tabasco sauce
pinch of dried oregano

Whisk all the ingredients together and refrigerate until ready to use. Just before serving, remove the garlic clove.

Serves 6
Per burger:

Calories: 309
Fat 10 g

Annette Funicello Italian Burgers

Oh, Annette, the queen of the beach party scene. We couldn't do a pool party menu without paying tribute to the ultimate bikini gal.

> 1 lb (500 g) lean ground turkey
> 1 cup (250 mL) crushed corn flakes
> 1 onion, finely minced
> 1/4 cup (50 mL) low- or non-fat Italian salad
>   dressing
> 1 tsp (5 mL) paprika
> 1/2 tsp (2 mL) dried Italian seasoning
> 1/8 tsp (0.5 mL) black pepper
> 1 clove garlic, finely minced

Preheat grill, 10 minutes for gas or propane and until coals glow beneath a white ash for charcoal.

In a large bowl, combine all the ingredients and mix well. Shape the mixture into 6 patties about 1/2-inch (1 cm) thick. Moisten your hands lightly with cold water while shaping patties and they won't stick to you. Lightly oil the grill and place patties on it over medium heat on gas grill or about 4 to 6 inches (10 to 15 cm) from coals over charcoal. Cook burgers about 5 minutes per side, or until cooked completely through.

The Skinny on Perfect Burgers

Never overmix the ground meat and your burgers will come out juicy every time.

Cluck It Up
Chicken Burgers

Serves 6

Per serving:

Calories: 288
Fat: 8 g

When you switch to ground chicken for your burgers, you can dramatically cut down on fat. Just make sure the package you buy at the market says "lean ground chicken" with a fat content of 10% or less.

> 1 1/2 lb (675 g) lean ground chicken
> 1/4 cup (50 mL) chopped red onion
> 2 tbsp (30 mL) chopped fresh parsley
> 1 1/2 tsp (7 mL) chopped fresh tarragon
> salt and pepper to taste
> 1/8 tsp (0.5 mL) dried thyme

Combine all the ingredients in a large bowl and mix well. Shape into 6 patties.

Heat the grill and lightly oil grill rack. Place the patties on rack and grill over medium heat on a gas grill or 4 to 6 inches (10 to 15 cm) from coals on a charcoal grill. Cook 4 minutes per side or until cooked through.

The Skinny on Thyme

Got time to try a new thyme? This herb packs a flavor wallop, and there's a whole range of varieties. English thyme brews into a lovely herb tea. French thyme goes great in casseroles. German winter thyme loves fish dishes, while caraway thyme adds a boost when chopped and sprinkled on a salad. There's even spicy nutmeg thyme, lemon thyme and oregano thyme for Italian and Greek foods.

Makes 2½ cups (675 mL)

Per serving (1 tbsp/15 mL):

Calories: 15
Fat: 0 g

Cranberry Ketchup

Here's our twist on an old favorite. Great on chicken burgers and sandwiches.

1 12-oz (375 g) bag fresh or frozen cranberries
1/3 cup (75 mL) maple syrup
1/3 cup (75 mL) granulated sugar
2 tbsp (30 mL) cider vinegar
2 tbsp (30 mL) finely chopped onion
1 tsp (5 mL) red pepper flakes
1/2 tsp (2 mL) salt
1/8 tsp (0.5 mL) ground allspice
1/8 tsp (0.5 mL) ground cloves
1/8 tsp (0.5 mL) pepper
1/8 tsp (0.5 mL) celery seed
1/8 tsp (0.5 mL) crushed mustard seed
1/2 bay leaf

In a large, heavy-bottomed saucepan, mix all the ingredients and simmer over medium-low heat, stirring frequently, for 10 to 15 minutes until cranberries have burst and mixture has thickened. Remove from heat. Cool, cover and chill until ready to serve. Will keep up to 2 weeks in the refrigerator.

Rainbow Pepper Relish

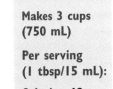

Makes 3 cups
(750 mL)

Per serving
(1 tbsp/15 mL):

Calories: 12
Fat: 0 g

This spicy relish is so colorful, it adds a festive touch to any table.
Great with Dive-in Pita Chips, baked tortilla chips, rolled up with
Yogo cheese on a flour tortilla, slathered on burgers and sand-
wiches — face it, it's good with anything.

> 1 large red pepper, finely diced
> 1 large green pepper, finely diced
> 1 large yellow pepper, finely diced
> 1 small hot pepper, finely minced
> 1 1/2 cups (375 mL) finely chopped red onion
> 2/3 cup (150 mL) white wine vinegar
> 1/2 cup (125 mL) granulated sugar
> 1/4 cup (50 mL) chopped coriander
> 1 tsp (5 mL) salt

Put the peppers and onions in a stainless steel or heavy enamelled
pan. Add water just to cover and bring to a boil. Cook for 5 minutes and drain in a colander.

Return the peppers and onions to the pan and add remaining
ingredients. Bring the mixture to a simmer over low heat and cook
for 5 minutes more. Remove from heat and cool. Store, covered,
in the refrigerator.

Serves 6

Per serving:

Calories: 12
Fat: 0 g

Splish Splash Lemon Ice

This refreshing dessert is perfect on a hot summer day. It looks especially nice served in large wine goblets. A few berries tossed on top makes a great variation.

> 1 cup (250 mL) boiling water
> 1 package (4-serving size) lemon-flavored,
>   sugar-free gelatin
> 1 cup (250 mL) chilled lemon-lime seltzer or soda
> 1/4 cup (50 mL) fresh lemon juice
> 1/2 tsp (2 mL) grated lemon zest
> few sprigs fresh mint for garnish

In a bowl, stir the boiling water into the gelatin until it dissolves. Stir in the seltzer, lemon juice and lemon zest.

Pour the mixture into a 9-inch (22 cm) square pan and cover. Freeze for 3 hours until solid. Let stand at room temperature for 10 minutes before putting mixture in a blender. Purée just a few seconds. Spoon into serving glasses and garnish with a mint sprig.

Strawberry Blonde Shortcake

Serves 10

Per serving:

Calories: 250
Fat: 7 g

Strawberry shortcake is one of those desserts that just says "summer." It also says "high fat" in its original form, but we've come up with a recipe that tastes just like the old-fashioned kind with none of the guilt. Our shortcake says "buy smaller size shorts."

> 3 cups (750 mL) sliced strawberries
> 2 tbsp (30 mL) granulated sugar
> 1 tbsp (15 mL) fresh lemon juice
> 2 cups (500 mL) all-purpose flour
> 2 tbsp (30 mL) granulated sugar
> 1 tbsp (15 mL) baking powder
> 1/4 tsp (1 mL) salt
> 1/3 cup (75 mL) margarine
> 3/4 cup (175 mL) skim milk

Combine the strawberries, sugar and lemon juice in a bowl and set aside.

In another bowl, combine the flour, sugar, baking powder and salt. Using two knives, or a pastry blender, cut in margarine until the mixture resembles coarse crumbs. Stir in the milk until just moistened. Do not overmix. Gather mixture into a ball and knead gently for about 20 seconds. Pat dough onto a lightly floured board to about 3/4 inch (2 cm) thick.

Using a 2 inch (5 cm) round cookie cutter or drinking glass, cut out 10 rounds and place them on a baking sheet. Bake at 350°F (180°C) for 12 to 15 minutes. Remove and let cool slightly.

To serve, split each biscuit in half and top with some of the strawberries.

Serve with low-fat frozen yogurt or low-fat whipped topping.

Serves 6

Per serving:

Calories: 50
Fat: trace

Grill 'Em Danno Grilled Pineapple

Maybe if the bad guys had known about this delicious dessert, there wouldn't have been any crime on Hawaii Five-O. The sugar caramelizes under the grill and adds a layer of spicy sweetness to the tropical fruit waiting beneath a smoosh of cream. Yum!

> **1 fresh pineapple**
> **1/2 cup (125 mL) non-fat sour cream**
> **brown sugar**
> **cinnamon**

Peel the pineapple and cut it in half. Core and cut each half in 1/2-inch (1.25 cm) slices.

Coat each slice with the sour cream and sprinkle with a little sugar and cinnamon.

Heat the broiler.

Put the slices on a broiler pan and broil on one side for 3 to 5 minutes until golden and bubbly.

The Skinny on a Diet That Works

Here's what to avoid if you're looking for a new diet. Drop the plan if:

1. Calories are too low. Women need at least 1,500 calories daily.
2. It's boring. You need variation in your diet for both your sanity and your health.
3. It's too complicated. You won't be able to stick with it.
4. It's nutritionally unbalanced. Too much of one kind of food is no good.
5. It claims you don't need to exercise. Oh yes, you do. For healthy heart and lungs and to lose weight, exercise is crucial.
6. It makes wild promises. Remember, if it sounds too good to be true, it is.
7. It says you'll lose 10 pounds (4.5 kg) in 10 days. No more than 2 pounds (0.9 kg) a week is a safe weight loss that can be kept off. Losing more can be dangerous, and may likely be just water.

∽∂ ∽∂ ∽∂ ∽∂ ∽∂ ∽∂ ∽∂ ∽∂ ∽∂ ∽∂ ∽∂ ∽∂ ∽∂ ∽∂ ∽∂ ∽∂ ∽∂ ∽∂

Fridge Raid!

It's 3 a.m. Do you know where your cookies are? Here's a super-skinny version of a cookie classic that weighs in at just 31 calories per cookie, and has a mere 1.1 grams of fat. A couple of these and a glass of skim milk and you've got a midnight snack for just 130 skinny calories.

Wendy and Barb's Midnight Raid Cookies

> 2 egg whites (at room temperature)
> 1/8 tsp (0.5 mL) cream of tartar
> 1/2 cup (125 mL) granulated sugar
> 2 1/2 cups (750 mL) corn flakes
> 2/3 cup (150 mL) loosely-packed shredded coconut
> 1/3 cup (75 mL) chopped walnuts
> 1/4 cup (50 mL) raisins

Heat oven to 300°F (150°C).

Line a cookie sheet with parchment paper. Beat the egg whites with the cream of tartar to soft peaks. Add the sugar and beat until stiff, but not dry. Fold in the cereal, coconut, nuts and raisins until all ingredients are coated.

Drop by rounded spoons onto the parchment. Bake for 20 to 25 minutes, or until light brown. Cool. These cookies only keep for about 4 days, but freeze well.

Chapter 6

Olé Mexican Spread

Menu

Cozumel Crunch Crackers
Tijuana Sunset Bean Dip
My Sister s Salsa
Broccomoli
Salad with Cool n Caliente Dressing
Hearty Black Bean Soup with Tortilla Strips
Lorne s Jalape o Cornbread
Sombrero Shrimp Fajitas
Aztec Mosaic Corn and Pepper Saut
La Bamba Spicy Rice
Chicken Mole
Tres Alarm Chili Con Carne
Sugar-Cinnamon Crispas with Strawberries

Introduction

You know the best time to have a bunch of pals over for a Mexican spread? The dead of winter. Nothing gets people over those February blahs like a piñata to swing at (great stress buster), some mariachi music and a big platter of Sombrero Shrimp Fajitas with plenty of Lorne's Jalapeño Cornbread to sop up the delicious juices.

If you come to our places for a party, chances are the theme will be Mexican, no matter what the season, and you'll find big bowls of My Sister's Salsa everywhere, thanks to Wendy's sis, Jan. People can't get enough of it, which is why we're sharing the recipe with you. And since Mexican is Barb's absolute favorite kind of food, you can bet all these recipes are fabulous.

Yes, we love south-of-the-border cuisine. We learned early on that salsa contains very few calories and no fat, so it became a big part of changing our eating habits 103 pounds ago. A dollop of salsa on a baked potato, cumin sprinkled on a turkey sandwich and a splash of hot sauce adds flavor, heat, but no sin to your foods. Buy a few and try them out — not all are blisteringly hot.

The problem with so many other Mexican foods is that, although they're delicious, they're also loaded with fat, either from being deep-fried or using lard in the preparation of the dish. This is not good for those of us wanting to lie on the beach at Cozumel in a bikini. Coming up with low-fat versions of our Mexican favorites was essential, because we had no intention of giving up these wonderful flavors. We were fat, not nuts.

Just a word to those who may like it hot, but find the fire down below a little tough to tame. You might want to serve a plain rice dish with this spread, using white rice, wild rice or a combination of both, simply cooked in a vegetable broth with no added flavorings. Also, a basket of warmed tortillas served alongside your main dishes would be an excellent way for your guests to control the burn.

The culprit is the capsicum in the peppers. If you get a blast furnace going in your mouth, the very best way to cool things off in a hurry is with a few sips of milk, a spoon of yogurt or sour cream. Believe us, it works.

You could also cut back on or omit the peppers, chili powder and hot sauces. But then, an extra spicy feast is one of those things that tastes so great and hurts so good. Maybe we should all turn up the heat once in awhile.

♈ Cocktails

Although cold Mexican beer with a squeeze of lime is probably the best drink to have with a Mexican feast, nothing compares with the sweet/salt/tart tang of a Margarita with a bowl of chips and salsa. There are more ways to make it than you can name, and, just like Martini drinkers, purists always insist theirs is the best way. Here's our favorite.

Commemorativo Margarita

Pre-mix recipe:

> 5 oz (150 mL) fresh lime juice
> 2 1/2 oz (75 mL) fresh lemon juice
> 5 oz (150 mL) water
> 1 tbsp (15 mL) granulated sugar

Mix all ingredients thoroughly.

Margarita

> 3 oz (60 mL) pre-mix
> 1 1/2 oz (35 mL) Commemorativo Tequila
> 1/2 oz (10 mL) Cointreau
> salt for rimming glasses

Dip the rim of a chilled glass into water, then into a bowl of salt. Fill halfway with ice. In a cocktail shaker, mix all liquid ingredients over ice. Pour into the glass and serve.

Wine Suggestions
White Zinfandel

Music Picks

From Wendy

Alex Fox, *Fly Away.* Shaibari.

From Barb

Gypsy Kings, *Greatest Hits.* Columbia.

**Makes about
100 crackers**

**Per serving
(5 crackers):**

**Calories: 96
Fat: 0.6 g**

Cozumel Crunch Crackers

The problem with crackers is that they're often loaded with fat. Solution? Make your own. These little hombres are so crispy-crunchy good, with virtually no fat, we may put a certain Mister out of business.

> 1 cup (250 mL) all-purpose flour
> 1 cup (250 mL) whole wheat flour
> 1/2 cup (125 mL) cracked wheat (bulgar)
> 1/2 cup (125 mL) sesame seeds
> 1 tbsp (15 mL) granulated sugar
> 1/2 tsp (2 mL) salt
> 1/2 tsp (2 mL) baking soda
> 1/4 cup (50 mL) margarine
> 3/4 cup (175 mL) buttermilk
> 1 egg white
> 1 tbsp (15 mL) water
> 2 tbsp (30 mL) poppy seeds

Preheat oven to 400°F (200°C).

In a large bowl, combine the all-purpose flour, whole wheat flour, cracked wheat, sesame seeds, sugar, salt and baking soda. With two knives or a pastry blender, cut in the margarine. Add the buttermilk and mix well.

Divide dough into 6 balls, each about the size of an egg. Roll each out on a lightly floured board into very thin (1/16 inch/2 mm) circles. Very carefully transfer them to an ungreased baking sheet.

In a small bowl, combine the egg white and water. Whisk lightly. Brush egg white mixture over each circle, then sprinkle the poppy seeds on top. Bake for about 10 minutes until lightly browned. Transfer to a wire rack to cool and crisp. Break into pieces and place in a basket beside your favorite dip or spread. If not using right away, store in an airtight container.

The Skinny on Fighting a Cold

Got the sniffles? Hot, spicy foods such as the ones you'll find in our Olé Mexico spread can actually help cold sufferers feel better. Just like a hot soup opens up your nasal passages and makes breathing easier, so do hot peppers help stuffy heads because they contain mucokinetic agents that get your nose running, eyes watering, and lungs opening up. So think olé when you say achoo!

Makes
1¹/₂ **cups**
(375 mL)

Per serving
(1 tbsp/15 mL):

Calories: 15
Fat: 0 g

Tijuana Sunset Bean Dip

Unlike the standard black bean variety, this dip has a lovely deep red color, thanks to the kidney beans and tomato paste. The lime juice adds a terrific tartness. And it's fat-free. Yippee! We think this may be your new favorite.

> 1 1/2 cups (375 mL) cooked or canned kidney
>   beans, drained
> 1/4 cup (50 mL) water
> 1 tbsp (15 mL) tomato paste
> 1 tbsp (15 mL) lime or lemon juice
> 1 tsp (5 mL) ground cumin
> 1/2 tsp (2 mL) dried oregano
> 1/4 tsp (1 mL) Tabasco sauce
> pinch cinnamon

In a food processor or blender, blend all ingredients until smooth. Place in a serving dish surrounded by homemade crackers or pita chips. You can find that recipe on page 95.

Back By Popular Demand... My Sister's Salsa

Makes 12 cups

Per serving
(4 tbsp/60 mL):

Calories: 19
Fat: 0.2 g

Jan's salsa is always a hit at parties. It's easy to make and once you've tried it, you may never go back to store-bought salsa again. We make up weekly batches and use it in everything. Barb just eats it straight from the bowl with extra lashings of hot sauce, of course.

> 5 cups (1.25 L) Italian plum tomatoes, peeled and chopped
> 3 cups (750 mL) mixed sweet peppers, chopped
> 1 cup (250 mL) chopped red and white onions
> 1 cup (250 mL) peeled, seeded, and chopped cucumbers
> 1 cup (250 mL) fresh coriander with stems, finely chopped
> 2 cloves garlic, finely chopped
> 3/4 cup (175 mL) tomato paste
> 1/4 cup (50 mL) fresh lime juice
> 1/4 cup (50 mL) red wine vinegar
> 1/2 tbsp (7 mL) salt
> Scotch bonnet peppers, finely chopped: 1=mild, 2=medium, 3=Wow! 4=Barb (And don't forget to wear gloves to do the chopping!)

Combine all the ingredients in a large bowl and store in the refrigerator until ready to use. Will keep up to 2 weeks. Use as a dip for chips and crackers or as a condiment with main dishes.

**Makes 2 cups
(500 mL)**

**Per serving
(2 tbsp/30 mL):**

Calories: 32
Fat: I g

Broccomoli

It's got a weird name, but this stuff is so good, you'll call it fantastic. Spicy, creamy and pretty thanks to the broccoli, it goes great on fajitas, as a dip, sandwich spread or condiment.

1 tomato, seeded and diced
2 cloves garlic, minced
1/4 cup (50 mL) finely chopped green onions
1 jalapeño, seeded, membrane removed and
   minced (wear gloves!)
2 tbsp (30 mL) lime juice
1/3 cup (80 mL) chopped fresh coriander
1/2 tsp (2 mL) salt
1 cup (250 mL) light ricotta cheese
1 cup (250 mL) cooked broccoli, coarsely puréed
   in a blender

Combine tomato, garlic, green onions, jalapeño, lime juice, coriander, and salt.

Add ricotta and mix well to combine all ingredients into a paste. Add broccoli and stir to combine.

The Skinny on Who's Hot

Not sure which chilies you should be cooking with? Most often, you'll
see a sign at the store telling you if they're mild, medium or hot, but it
can be hard to predict. As a rule of thumb, poblano chilies are the
mildest, followed by jalapeños and banana peppers in the middle. Scotch
bonnets and habañeros are the ones you need asbestos gloves to handle.
They're seriously hot, so go easy, unless you're like Barb and can't get enough of the stuff.

Salad with Cool 'n' Caliente Dressing

Serves 8

**Per serving
(2 tbsp/30 mL):**

**Calories: 20
Fat: 0.1 g**

"Caliente" is Spanish for hot, because this dressing packs a kick in a cool creamy base. We also like it as a dip for veggies.

8 cups (2 L) mixed salad greens

Dressing:
1 cup (250 mL) plain non-fat yogurt
3 tbsp (45 mL) skim milk
1 tbsp (15 mL) jalapeño, minced finely (you
   know the drill, wear gloves)
1 clove garlic, minced finely
1/4 tsp (1 mL) ground cumin
1/8 tsp (0.5 mL) salt

Put all dressing ingredients in a jar with a tight-fitting lid. Shake well to combine and refrigerate until ready to use. Toss with greens.

Serves 4

Per serving:

Calories: 260
Fat: 4g

Hearty Black Bean Soup with Tortilla Strips

Using canned black beans makes whipping up this delicious, rib-sticking soup a snap. And the tortilla strips add a unique flavor. Try corn tortillas for a completely different taste. Rich, satisfying, this is one of our favorites. Add a dollop of low-fat sour cream on top of each serving if you like, but remember you'll add a few calories and a trace of fat.

4 6-inch (15 cm) flour tortillas, cut in strips
2 tsp (10 mL) olive oil
6 green onions, sliced
2 cloves garlic, minced
1 green pepper, diced
2 jalapeño peppers, seeded and membrane removed (gloves, please)
1 tbsp (15 mL) chili powder
1 19-oz (540 mL) can stewed tomatoes, chopped with juice
2 19-oz (540 mL) cans black beans, rinsed and drained
2 cups (500 mL) vegetable broth
1 cup (250 mL) water
3/4 cup (175 mL) chopped fresh coriander
2 tbsp (30 mL) lime juice

Place tortilla strips on a baking sheet and bake in a 375°F (190°C) oven for about 5 minutes or until crisp.

In a large saucepan, heat the oil. Add the green onions and garlic and cook, stirring, about 3 minutes. Add the green pepper, the jalapeños and the chili powder and cook, stirring, another 5 minutes. Add the tomatoes and juice, the beans, broth, water, and half the coriander. Reduce heat and simmer for 15 minutes.

Remove soup from the heat and add the lime juice. Ladle into soup bowls and garnish with the remaining coriander and the tortilla strips.

The Skinny on Soup

The French say a good soup smiles as it simmers. We love that idea, that something as simple as aroma can lift people's spirits. But it's true. Watch your guests' faces when they walk in and sniff the fabulous scents wafting from a simmering pot of soup on your stove. Is it possible to taste love? We think so.

Lorne's Jalapeño Cornbread

Our close friend Lorne is a real hot guy, especially when it comes to his bread!

1 cup (250 mL) cornmeal
1 cup (250 mL) all-purpose flour
1 tsp (5 mL) baking powder
1/2 tsp (2 mL) baking soda
3/4 tsp (3 mL) salt
1 tbsp (15 mL) brown sugar
1/4 tsp cayenne
pepper to taste
1 cup (250 mL) creamed corn
3/4 cup (175 mL) frozen corn kernels
1/2 cup (125 mL) non-fat sour cream
1/2 cup (125 mL) skim milk
1 egg
1 egg white, lightly beaten
2 tbsp (30 mL) vegetable oil
3 jalapeño peppers, chopped

Preheat oven to 400°F (200°C). Lightly grease a 13 x 9-inch (3.5 L) baking pan and set aside.

Mix all dry ingredients. In a separate bowl, mix all wet ingredients. Fold dry ingredients into wet mixture. Don't overmix. Pour batter into prepared pan. Bake for 25 to 30 minutes until golden brown.

Sombrero Shrimp Fajitas

Everybody loves fajitas. They're fun to put together and eat, even if they can get sloppy. That's when they're best. We're suggesting you use a Mexican vegetable called jicama to garnish your fajitas. It looks like a brown baseball, flattened on both ends, and tastes, well, much better than a brown baseball. Think of the texture of radishes but very, very mild and slightly sweet.

> 1 1/2 lb (750 g), shrimp, cleaned and deveined
> (you can also substitute scallops or chicken)
> 2 tbsp (30 mL) lime juice
> 2 tbsp (30 mL) water
> 1 tsp (5 mL) ground cumin
> 1 tsp (15 mL) chili powder
> 1 jalapeño seeded, membrane removed, finely
> minced (you will wear gloves, won't you?)
> 2 tsp (10 mL) olive oil
> 1 clove garlic, finely minced
> 1 green pepper, sliced in strips
> 1 red pepper, sliced in strips
> 2 onions, sliced into thin rings
> 8 10-inch (25 cm) tortillas
> 2 cups (500 mL) shredded lettuce
> 1/4 cup (50 mL) chopped fresh coriander
> 1 cup (250 mL) peeled and diced jicama

Mix together the lime juice, water, cumin, chili powder and jalapeño in a shallow dish. Add the shrimp. Cover and marinate in the refrigerator for 30 minutes.

Heat the oil in a heavy skillet and add the garlic, peppers and onions. Sauté over medium-high heat, tossing frequently, until vegetables start to soften. Add the shrimp and about 2 tablespoons (30 mL) of the marinade. Quickly sauté until the shrimp are pink and just cooked, about 4 minutes.

Stack the tortillas on top of each other and wrap in aluminum foil. Warm in a preheated 350°F (180°C) oven for 5 to 10 minutes, or wrap in a damp paper towel and microwave for 30 seconds.

To serve, place some of the shrimp mixture down the middle of each tortilla. Top with a little lettuce, coriander, and jicama. Roll up and enjoy!

My Sister's Salsa goes great with this, as does the Broccomoli.

Aztec Mosaic Corn and Pepper Sauté

Serves 4

Per serving:

Calories: 80
Fat: 1.2 g

This bright and colorful vegetable dish looks terrific on your table. You'll want to serve it when any meal needs a bit of a boost.

> 2 tsp (10 mL) olive oil
> 1 red pepper, diced
> 1 green pepper, diced
> 1 red onion, diced
> 1 clove garlic, minced
> 1/2 cup (125 mL) vegetable broth
> 1 10-oz (300 g) package frozen corn
> salt and pepper to taste
> 2 tbsp (30 mL) chopped fresh coriander

Heat the oil in a large skillet. Add the peppers, onion and garlic, and sauté for about 5 minutes until vegetables start to soften. Add the broth and bring to a boil. Reduce heat to a simmer and stir in the corn, salt, pepper and half the coriander. Cook for 2 to 3 minutes more. Put the corn mixture into a serving bowl and sprinkle the remaining coriander over the top.

La Bamba Spicy Rice

La Bamba is the rattlesnake made famous in the song by Latin rocker Richie Valens. The rattlesnake hiding in this dish is the jalapeño. But don't worry. It won't bite. Much.

> 2 tsp (10 mL) olive oil
> 1 onion, finely chopped
> 2 cloves garlic, minced
> 1 jalapeño, seeded, and minced (and what are
>   you wearing?)
> 1/2 tsp (2 mL) ground cumin
> 1 cup (250 mL) long grain rice
> 1 3/4 cups (425 mL) vegetable broth
> salt and pepper to taste
> 1/4 cup (50 mL) chopped fresh parsley
>   or coriander

Heat oil in a large non-stick saucepan. Add the onion, garlic, jalapeño and cumin. Sauté over low heat, stirring frequently, for about 4 minutes. Add the rice and stir to combine ingredients. Sauté for 1 minute more. Add the broth and bring to a boil. Reduce heat and cover pan. Simmer for about 20 minutes, until rice is tender and all broth has been absorbed. Stir in chopped parsley or coriander and season with salt and pepper to taste.

Chicken Mole

Serves 4

Per serving:
Calories: 186
Fat: 5 g

This is the signature fiesta dish of Mexico. Mole (pronounced Mo-lay) is actually the name for any complicated, gourmet sauce. How complicated? Well, the traditional Mole Poblano can take three days to make. Our version takes considerably less time, and uses chicken instead of the classic turkey, but stays true to the spirit of mole by combining flavors like raisins, chili, tomato and chocolate. Yes, chocolate. This extraordinary, velvety, rich brown sauce tastes like nothing else. Give it a try.

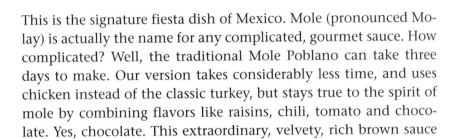

4 boneless, skinless chicken breasts
1 tsp (15 mL) olive oil
2 green onions, finely chopped
1 garlic clove, minced
1 tsp (5 mL) cocoa powder
1 tsp (5 mL) chili powder
1/2 tsp (2 mL) ground cumin
1 1/4 cups (300 mL) can tomato purée
2 tbsp (30 mL) raisins
1/4 cup (50 mL) water
2 tbsp (30 mL) chopped fresh coriander

Preheat oven to 400°F (200°C). Place the chicken breasts in a baking dish and set aside.

In a large non-stick saucepan, heat the oil. Add the green onions and garlic and sauté over medium heat for 1 minute. Add the cocoa, chili powder and cumin and cook, stirring, for 1 minute. Add the tomato purée, raisins, water and coriander and cook over low heat for about 10 minutes uncovered. Pour the sauce over the chicken and bake for 30 to 45 minutes until chicken is cooked through.

Serves 6

Per serving:

Calories: 251
Fat: 3g

Tres Alarm
Chili Con Carne

Can't have a Tex-Mex feed without chili, and we think you'll find our version is as tasty as the higher-fat recipes. A basket of warm tortillas and a green salad and you've got a great supper for the family or the gang.

1/3 cup (75 mL) vegetable broth
1 onion, diced
2 carrots, diced
1 stalk celery, sliced
1 clove garlic, minced
1 tbsp (15 mL) chili powder
1 tsp (5 mL) ground cumin
2 tbsp (30 mL) chopped fresh coriander
1 1/2 cups (375 mL) canned tomatoes, drained
    and chopped
1 4-oz (125 mL) can tomato paste
1 4-oz (125 mL) can green chilies, chopped
2 cups (500 mL) tomato juice
2 tbsp (30 mL) My Sister's Salsa
1 19-oz (540 mL) can red kidney beans
1 19-oz (540 mL) can pinto beans
1 lb (500 grams) lean flank steak, cut in
    1/2-inch (1 cm) pieces

In a large non-stick saucepan or Dutch oven, heat the broth. Add the onion, carrots, celery, garlic, chili powder, cumin and coriander. Sauté for about 5 minutes until vegetables begin to soften. Add the tomatoes and tomato paste and cook for 5 more minutes. Add the chilies, tomato juice, salsa, kidney beans, pinto beans and the steak. Cook for 1 hour over low heat, stirring occasionally.

Serves 6

Per serving:

Calories: 200
Fat: 0.3 g

Sugar-Cinnamon Crispas with Strawberries

A great, refreshing dessert guaranteed to cut some of the heat from your spread. Everybody loves these crispy-sweet treats with their cinnamon flavor. Perfect for scooping up frozen yogurt or low-fat ice cream.

> 2 pints (1 L) strawberries, washed, hulled
>   and sliced
> 2 tbsp (30 mL) granulated sugar
> 2 tsp (10 mL) cinnamon
> 18 wonton wrappers (3 inches/7.5 cm square)
> low or non-fat vanilla frozen yogurt,
>   or 1% ice cream

Preheat oven to 375°F (190°C). Place strawberries in a bowl and sprinkle 1 tablespoon (15mL) sugar over the top. Set aside.

In a small bowl, combine the cinnamon and remaining sugar. Set aside.

Bring a large pot of water to a boil. Add half of the wrappers to the water, 1 at a time.

Cook for 1 to 2 minutes, then remove with a slotted spoon to a bowl of ice water. Repeat with remaining wrappers.

Spray a large baking sheet with cooking spray and carefully transfer half the wrappers to it, laying them flat. Lightly spray wrappers with a little cooking spray, then sprinkle on the cinnamon sugar mixture. Bake for 15 to 18 minutes, or until crisp and golden brown. Remove to a wire baking rack to cool. Repeat with remaining wrappers.

To assemble, place a scoop of yogurt or 1% ice cream in a bowl, spoon some of the strawberries over the top and stick 3 of the crisps into the yogurt.

The Skinny on Low-Fat Cooking Skills

These add big taste without adding calories.

1. **Caramelizing.** Cook ingredients, most commonly onions, in a non-stick skillet until browned and very tender. After about 8 minutes, the onions will reach a rich caramel color and the flavor will be sweet and intense.

2. **Reducing.** Reducing cooking liquid evaporates water and leaves concentrated flavor. Add liquid like vegetable broth or wine to the browned ingredients in the bottom of a non-stick skillet after sautéing chicken, veggies or other meats. Remove the cooked food, add the liquid and bring to a boil. Scrape up the browned bits with a wooden spoon and cook until sauce reaches desired volume, usually half of what you started with.

3. **Flour Dredging and Browning.** Rinse chicken or fish. Pat dry with paper towels. Put all-purpose flour on a dinner plate and roll chicken or fish in it to coat. Shake off excess, and brown in a non-stick skillet over medium heat until lightly browned and crisp. Don't try to put too many pieces in the pan, or the food won't brown properly.

4. **To Skim Fat.** When simmering soup or stews, try laying a piece of paper towel across the surface of the pot to remove fat. A lettuce leaf also does the trick. And do invest in a fat-skimming measuring cup to separate fat from pan juices to make low-fat gravies for meats and poultry.

This page, clockwise from top:
Sombrero Shrimp Fajitas (p. 127)
Hearty Black Bean Soup with Tortilla Strips (p. 124)
Lorne's Jalapeño Cornbread (p. 126)
Sugar-Cinnamon Crispas with Strawberries (p. 134)
Salad with Cool 'n' Caliente Dressing (p. 123)
Aztec Mosaic Corn and Pepper Sauté (p. 129)
Broccomoli (p. 122)
Tijuana Sunset Bean Dip (p. 120)
My Sister's Salsa (p. 121)
Cozumel Crunch Crackers (p. 118)

Overleaf, clockwise from top:
Low-Fat Pesto Variations (p. 154)
Rock and Roma Lasagne (p. 151)
Aromatic Focaccia (p. 146)
Antipasti Platter (p. 142)

Chapter 7

Mama Mia Spread

Menu

Mediterranean Magic Tomato-Mozzarella Salad
Antipasti Platter
Aromatic Rosemary Focaccia
Wendy and Barb s Amore Appetizers
Napoli Shrimp and Pesto Pizzas
Rock and Roma Lasagne
Skinny Eggplant Parmigiana
Low-Fat Pesto Variations
Zucchini la Genovese
Gina Lollobrigida Chicken
Veal-y Delicious Piccata with Capers
Venus Sorbet
Apricot Biscotti

Introduction

Everybody adores Italian food, and we're no exception. With so many regions, each with its own unique cuisine, a tour of Italy would really be like a banquet or, as we like to say, a spread.

It's easy to think of the romantic Roman grotto look and menu to match when you plan an Italian spread. You know, red-checked tablecloths, straw Chianti bottles with candles, crusty bread and some guy singing about "Amore."

But the part we don't *amore* is the fat that is usually a mainstay of Italian recipes. True, except for northern cuisines where butter rules, the Italians generally rely on olive oil. Although that's a lot better for your heart and arteries, when it comes to zipping up those skin-tight Capri pants, your hips don't know the difference. Fat is fat.

We wanted to keep the "heart" in our hearty Mama Mia Spread by adapting the classics to make them healthy, as well as colorful and delicious, taking our favorite Italian foods, like lasagne and chicken Parmesan, and giving them a Wendy and Barb makeover. Rock and Roma Lasagne is a fun and funky dish where the noodles are rolled into spirals around a delicious spinach and low-fat cheese filling. Gina Lollobrigida Chicken uses all the same ingredients of the classic Parmigiana, but weighs in at just 230 calories and 7 grams of fat. We've even created some low-fat pesto variations, vibrant-hued creations for you to wow your guests with.

We love Italian food. Also, Italian cars, clothes and, especially, men. So get in the kitchen and let's *mangia*!

 Cocktails

Italians take their aperitifs seriously. Imagine sitting on a vine-covered balcony overlooking the hills of Rome at dusk, or on a tile terrace facing a Venetian canal as you sit and savor a Campari and soda or a red vermouth over ice with a twist of lemon.

This refreshing potion looks as lovely as a Tuscan sunset. Serve it with a platter of antipasti, some bruschetta and soft music in the background. Light the candles and say chin-chin.

St. Raphael Aperitif

3 oz (60 mL) St. Raphael Gold Wine Aperitif
3 oz (60 mL) ginger ale
3 oz (60 mL) cranberry juice
Splash lime juice
Strawberry for garnish

Fill a large, chilled balloon wine glass halfway with ice. Mix all ingredients in a shaker and pour into glass. Garnish with strawberry.

Wine Suggestions
Chianti or Sangiovese

Music Picks

Great minds think alike!
Both of us chose:

José Carreras, Placido Domingo, Luciano Pavarotti,
The Three Tenors, *Mehta*. London.

Work Out, Kid

Don't let your kids be your excuse for not exercising. Barb started running the track with one eye on baby Jake and the other on her route. Look for a gym that offers child care. Many do. Make being fit a family affair.

Mediterranean Magic Tomato-Mozzarella Salad

When summer tomatoes are at their peak, this is a heavenly dish. To always have fresh basil handy, why not grow a plant in your garden or in a pot in a sunny kitchen window?

> 1 tsp (5 mL) olive oil
> 1 tbsp (15 mL) balsamic vinegar
> 1 tbsp (15 mL) chopped fresh parsley
> 1 large beefsteak tomato or other firm,
>   ripe variety
> 4 thin slices part-skim mozzarella
> 4 to 6 basil leaves

Mix the oil, vinegar and parsley in a bowl. Set aside.

Slice tomato into 4 thick slices and place in the oil-vinegar mixture, turning to coat. Refrigerate for 30 minutes.

To assemble, place a tomato slice on a salad plate. Top with 1 slice mozzarella and 1 or 2 basil leaves. Sprinkle leftover marinade over the top, or a couple of drops of balsamic vinegar. Repeat with remaining tomato slices.

Antipasti Platter

◈ ━━━━━━━━━━━━━━━━━━━━━━━━━━━ ◈

Meaning "before the meal," a platter of antipasti served on a platter is a favorite way for Italian food lovers to nibble while they enjoy a drink and good conversation before the meal. Here's our healthy version of this Italian tradition. We've got three recipes for you to try. Make them all and wow your guests. They'll never guess this is a low-fat feast.

> **10 to 15 slices low-fat luncheon meats of your choice, such as ham, smoked turkey or any light spiced meat.**
> **10 to 15 slices low-fat sliced cheeses of your choice, such as provolone or mozzarella.**

Roll up meats and cheeses individually and place around the outside of a large platter. Arrange the following components (recipes are coming up) attractively on the inside of the platter.

Marinated Mushrooms and Artichokes

Serves 12

Per serving:

Calories: 39
Fat: 1 g

Marinade:
2/3 cup (150 mL) tarragon vinegar
1 tbsp (15 mL) olive oil
1 tbsp (15 mL) granulated sugar
1 tbsp (15 mL) fresh chopped basil
1 tsp (5 mL) dried oregano
3 tbsp (45 mL) vegetable broth
1 tbsp (15 mL) water
dash of Tabasco
1/4 tsp (1 mL) red pepper flakes
1 clove garlic, minced
salt and pepper to taste

In a large bowl, combine all ingredients and mix well.

1 1/2 lb (750 g) small mushrooms, cleaned
1 14-oz (398 mL) can artichoke hearts, drained,
    and halved or quartered
1 onion, sliced into thin rings

Add the vegetables to marinade and refrigerate overnight, stirring occasionally. Drain before adding to antipasti platter.

Serves 6

Per serving:

Calories: 28
Fat: 0.5 g

Roasted Peppers

2 red peppers
2 green peppers
1 tsp (5 mL) olive oil
2 tsp (10 mL) lemon juice
salt and pepper to taste
4 garlic cloves, cut in quarters

Place the peppers on a broiler rack and broil 4 inches (10 cm) from heat for about 15 minutes, turning every 3 to 4 minutes with tongs, until skin is blistered and charred. You can also grill them using a barbecue. Place peppers in a brown paper bag and seal, or place in a bowl and cover with a tea towel. Leave for 10 minutes.

Peel off skins, seed and remove membranes. Pat dry and cut in wide strips. Place in a shallow dish.

Whisk together the oil, lemon juice, salt, pepper and garlic. Pour over the peppers and refrigerate overnight, turning occasionally. Remove the garlic before adding peppers to platter and let come to room temperature for best flavor.

Marinated Seafood Salad

Serves 8

Per serving:

Calories: 170
Fat: 2.5 g

8 oz (250 g) small shrimp, peeled and deveined
8 oz (250 g) scallops
8 oz (250 g) squid, cleaned, body cut in rings,
   tentacles intact

In a saucepan, bring 4 cups (1 L) of water to a boil. Reduce heat and simmer. Add shrimp, scallops and squid and cook for 2 minutes, just until shrimp are pink and scallops and squid are opaque. Drain and rinse under cold water. Place in a shallow bowl and set aside.

Marinade:
3 tbsp (45 mL) red wine vinegar
1 tbsp (15 mL) olive oil
1/4 cup (50 mL) fresh lemon juice
1 clove garlic, minced
1 tsp (5 mL) dried basil
1 tsp (5 mL) dried oregano
salt and pepper to taste
2 tbsp (30 mL) chopped fresh parsley

Mix all ingredients together and pour over seafood. Cover and refrigerate for 30 minutes. Add to antipasti platter.

Serves 8

Per serving:

Calories: 250

Fat: 3 g

Aromatic Rosemary Focaccia

Love grows where my Rosemary goes, so the song says. Rosemary is one of those herbs that just sparkles in any dish, and on a soft, yeasty focaccia straight from the oven, it's heaven. Yes, this recipe takes awhile to make, but it's well worth the effort. And think of all the calories you'll burn kneading and punching that dough.

> 1 package (8 g) active dry yeast
> 2 tbsp (30 mL) granulated sugar
> 1 1/2 cups (375 mL) warm water
> 1 tsp (5 mL) salt
> 2 tsp (10 mL) olive oil
> 4 to 5 cups (1 to 1.25 L) all-purpose flour
> 3 tbsp (45 mL) cornmeal
>
> Topping:
> 2 tsp (10 mL) olive oil
> 1 1/2 tbsp (25 mL) chopped fresh rosemary
> 1/4 tsp (1 mL) fresh ground black pepper
> 1/4 tsp (1 mL) coarse salt

In a large bowl, combine the yeast, sugar and 6 tablespoons (90 mL) of the warm water. Let stand until the mixture becomes foamy, about 10 minutes.

Add the remaining warm water, salt and oil. Add the flour 1/2 cup (125 mL) at a time, until mixture starts to form a ball and comes away from the sides of the bowl.

Turn dough out onto a floured board and knead until dough

becomes smooth. That takes about 6 minutes. Put on some loud music and get rid of all your tensions by kneading the stuffing out of the dough.

Place the dough in a lightly oiled bowl and cover. Let it rise in a warm place free from drafts for 1 to 2 hours, until doubled in bulk. The oven (heat off, with the light on) is a good place.

While the dough is rising, combine the oil, rosemary, pepper and salt in a small bowl and set aside.

When dough has risen, punch it down in the bowl and turn it out onto a board.

Divide the dough in half and form into 2 even circles or rectangles.

Place the dough on a baking sheet that has been sprinkled with cornmeal. Cover again and let rise until doubled in size, about 1 hour.

Preheat the oven to 375°F (190°C). With your fingers, poke holes in the dough (not all the way through). Form a pattern, spell a name, make a picture, be creative. Spread the rosemary mixture evenly over each bread and bake for 20 to 30 minutes. Let it stand 10 minutes before serving and cut into squares or wedges.

Serves 10

Per serving:

Calories: 80
Fat: trace

Wendy and Barb's Amore Appetizers

Bruschetta (say it brew-sket-ta and sound like a native) makes a terrific, quick appetizer, but some versions call for great gobs of oil. Not for us. We practise what we preach, and eat what we make. Here's a great way to enjoy our "You Won't Believe This Is Low-Fat" Bruschetta.

> 1 loaf of best quality Italian bread, cut in 1/2-
> inch (1 cm) slices
> 2 to 3 cloves garlic, peeled and left whole
> 1 container (227 g) Wendy and Barb's "You
> Won't Believe This Is Low-Fat" Bruschetta

Preheat oven to 400°F (200°C). Place the slices of bread on a baking sheet and toast until lightly browned and crispy. Take one of the cloves of garlic and scrape on one side of the toasted bread (almost like you're grating the garlic). A little goes a long way. Unless you love garlic, in which case, go nuts. Repeat with remaining slices, using another clove as they are used up. Top with 2 teaspoons (10 mL) bruschetta and spread it over the bread. Place bread slices back on baking sheet and bake for 3 to 5 minutes more until just reheated.

Napoli Shrimp and Pesto Pizzas

Shrimp and our succulent sundried pesto. Now that's amore. We use the focaccia dough recipe for the pizza crust, but if you've got to have that pizza fix now, try one of the excellent frozen pizza doughs at the supermarket, or pre-packaged crusts from your bakery. Just remember to read the label and if the product is high in fat, give it a miss.

Sundried Tomato Pesto

1 cup (250 mL) sundried tomatoes (not packed in oil) soaked in warm water for 15 minutes, drained and chopped
1 clove garlic
2 tbsp (30 mL) balsamic vinegar
1 tbsp (15 mL) chopped fresh oregano
2 tsp (10 mL) olive oil
2 tsp (10 mL) vegetable broth
1/2 tsp (2 mL) grated orange zest
1/4 tsp (1 mL) salt
1/4 tsp (1 mL) pepper

Place all ingredients in a blender or food processor and purée until smooth.

Pizza Dough

Follow the recipe for focaccia on page 146 but after first rising, divide dough into 4 equal portions and shape into rounds. Place on cornmeal-coated baking sheet. Let rise 1 hour and bake for 20 to 30 minutes.

Topping

1 cup (250 mL) small shrimp, peeled, deveined, cooked and chopped coarsely. For a variation, slice whole shrimp in half lengthwise.
2 tsp (10 mL) Parmesan cheese
1 tbsp (15 mL) fresh basil, finely chopped

Preheat oven to 450°F (230°C). To assemble, take one focaccia pizza round, place 3 tablespoons (45 mL) of the pesto on it and spread it around with the back of a spoon. Sprinkle 1/4 cup (60 mL) of the cooked shrimp over or, if using slices, lay them on top. Sprinkle on a little of the Parmesan and a little of the basil. Repeat with remaining pizzas. Bake for 3 to 5 minutes or until hot.

The Skinny on Pizza

No, pizza isn't the enemy. In fact, it's one of the best fast-food choices you can make. Although a single slice can weigh in at 25 grams of fat, you can do better if you order smart. Avoid crispy crusts as they usually contain oil. Ask if your pie can be made with low-fat cheese. And skip the fatty meats like pepperoni and bacon and ask for a veggie delight. Or do what Barb does — order double veggies, hold the mozzarella and substitute a sprinkle of Parmesan. Also, check out your supermarket. Some freezer pizzas contain fewer than 10 grams of fat per slice.

Rock and Roma Lasagne

Serves 4
Per serving:
Calories: 400
Fat: 6 g

Everybody loves lasagne, but there has to be a way to enjoy all those flavors without the calorie overload. Here's Wendy and Barb to the rescue with a nifty new way of making the dish that not only cuts the fat and calories, but also has an updated look. This Italian fashion is straight from our kitchen runway. And the look for this season is delicious, bella.

> 8 lasagne noodles
> 1 tsp (5 mL) olive oil
> 1 onion, finely chopped
> 2 cloves garlic, minced
> 1 large carrot, finely diced
> 1 10-oz (284 g) package frozen spinach thawed,
>   chopped and all moisture squeezed out
> 3/4 cup (175 mL) 1% cottage cheese
> 3 tbsp (45 mL) Parmesan cheese
> salt and pepper to taste
> 1 egg white, lightly beaten
> 1 19-oz (540 mL) can stewed tomatoes, with juice
> 1 cup (250 mL) tomato sauce
> fresh chopped parsley for garnish

Cook noodles according to package directions. Drain them and put in a bowl of cold water.

In a non-stick skillet, heat the oil. Add the onion, garlic and carrot and sauté for about 8 minutes, or until vegetables begin to soften. Add the spinach and sauté over medium heat for another 4 minutes.

Transfer mixture to a large mixing bowl and cool.

To the spinach mixture, add the cottage cheese, Parmesan, salt, pepper and the egg white. Stir to combine well.

Preheat oven to 400°F (200°C). To assemble, place a noodle flat on a work surface and top with 3 tablespoons (45 mL) of the spinach mixture; spread out almost to edges. Roll up jelly-roll style from the narrow end. Place rolls seam-side down in a baking dish that has been lightly sprayed with cooking spray. Repeat with remaining noodles.

Mix the tomatoes and tomato sauce together and spoon over roll-ups. Cover with aluminum foil and bake for about 10 minutes. Uncover and bake for an additional 10 minutes.

To serve, place two of the roll-ups on a dinner plate, spoon some of the sauce over and sprinkle with the chopped parsley.

Skinny Eggplant Parmigiana

Serves 4

Per serving:

Calories: 200
Fat: 3 g

Eggplant acts like a sponge, so you have to watch the amount of oil you use to fry it. Our skinny recipe uses tomatoes to keep the eggplant moist and it makes for a de-lightful variation on other high-fat eggplant dishes.

> 1 medium eggplant, cut in 1/2-inch (1 cm) dice
> 1 tsp (5 mL) olive oil
> 1 onion, chopped finely
> 3 cloves garlic, minced
> salt and pepper to taste
> 1 19-oz (540 mL) can diced tomatoes, with 1/2
>   cup (125 mL) juice reserved
> 1 bay leaf
> 1 tsp (5 mL) dried oregano
> 2 tbsp (30 mL) Parmesan cheese
> 1/2 cup (125 mL) shredded part-skim mozzarella
> 2 tbsp (30 mL) chopped fresh parsley

In a large skillet, heat the oil. Add the onion and garlic and sauté over medium heat for 2 minutes. Add the eggplant, salt and pepper and sauté for another 2 minutes. Add the tomatoes and the reserved juice, along with the bay leaf and oregano. Heat over high heat until bubbling. Lower heat and simmer for 20 minutes, stirring often, until eggplant is tender. Discard the bay leaf and transfer mixture to a baking dish. Sprinkle Parmesan, mozzarella and parsley over the top and bake in a 350°F (180°C) oven for about 10 minutes, or until cheese has melted and casserole is hot and bubbly.

Low-Fat Pesto Variations

Pesto, with its intense flavors of basil and garlic, is a delectable way to dress pasta, perk up a sandwich, add a boost to spaghetti sauce or add pizzazz to a pizza. But the amount of oil in most pesto recipes would leave anybody's toga too tight. No problem, we've found a way to cut the fat and keep all the flavor. And we even have a couple of versions for you to try.

Makes 1¼ cups (300 mL)

Per serving (¼ cup/50 mL):

Calories: 47
Fat: 1.5 g

Basil Pesto

1 cup (250 mL) loosely packed basil leaves
1 to 2 garlic cloves, peeled
1 1/2 cups (375 mL) chopped zucchini
1/3 cup (75 mL) chicken broth
1/4 cup (50 mL) Parmesan cheese
1/2 tsp (2 mL) salt

In a food processor or blender, blend all ingredients into a smooth purée.

Rosy Roasted Red Pepper Pesto

Makes ³/₄ cup (180 mL)

Per serving (3 tbsp/45 mL):
Calories: 50
Fat: 1.7g

1 8-oz (250 g) jar roasted red peppers, drained
1 clove garlic
1 tbsp (15 mL) olive oil
1/2 tbsp (7 mL) chopped fresh rosemary
salt and pepper to taste

Combine all ingredients in a food processor or blender and purée until smooth.

Santa Fe Pesto

Makes ¹/₂ cup (125 mL)

Per serving (2 tbsp/30 mL):
Calories: 59
Fat: 2 g

1 cup (250 mL) loosely packed coriander leaves
1 oz (25 g) grated Monterey Jack cheese
2 tbsp (30 mL) lime juice
1 jalapeño pepper, seeded and chopped (wear gloves for this)
1 clove garlic
1 tsp (5 mL) grated lime zest
salt and pepper to taste

Put all ingredients in a food processor or a blender and purée until smooth. Goes great with grilled chicken, too.

Serve any of these pestos tossed with your favorite hot, drained pasta in place of a sauce. The combinations are virtually endless, so experiment. Let us know what you come up with.

Serves 4

Per serving:
Calories: 58
Fat: 1.8 g

Zucchini à la Genovese

The Ligurian coast of Northern Italy, which is home to Genoa, is where pesto was born. These smart folks knew that basil and garlic were made to be together. We think so, too, and when you toss some zucchini in there, you've got a classic side dish.

> 2 tsp (10 mL) soft margarine
> 2 cloves garlic, minced
> 4 small zucchini, sliced
> 1 tbsp (15 mL) lemon juice
> salt and pepper to taste
> 1/4 cup (50 mL) chopped fresh parsley
> 2 tbsp (30 mL) chopped fresh basil

Heat the margarine in a large non-stick skillet. Add the garlic and sauté over medium-high heat for 1 minute. Add the zucchini, lemon juice, salt and pepper and sauté for 5 to 6 minutes until the zucchini is tender-crisp. Add the parsley and basil and cook for 30 seconds more. Serve hot.

Gina Lollobrigida Chicken

Serves 4

Per serving:

Calories: 240
Fat: 7 g

Gina Lollobrigida, now there's an Italian dish. She set the standard for sultry, sexy glamor in the late '50s. We've named this Italian classic after her.

> 2 egg whites
> 1 tbsp (15 mL) skim milk
> 1/3 cup (75 mL) bread crumbs
> 1/3 cup (75 mL) Parmesan cheese
> 1 tsp (5 mL) dried oregano
> 1/4 tsp (1 mL) black pepper
> 4 boneless, skinless chicken breasts, pounded to
>   1/4-inch (1 cm) thickness
> 1 large tomato, diced
> 4 small slices part-skim mozzarella

In a small bowl, whisk together the egg and milk.

On a plate, mix together the bread crumbs, Parmesan, oregano and pepper.

Dip each chicken breast in the egg mixture, then dredge in the bread crumb mixture. Shake off excess and set on a clean plate.

Spray a skillet with cooking spray and heat over medium-high heat. Place chicken breasts in skillet and cook for 3 to 4 minutes per side. Transfer chicken to a casserole dish. Top each chicken breast with 1/4 of the tomatoes and a slice of the mozzarella. Broil for 1 to 2 minutes 3 to 4 inches (7.5 to 10 cm) from heat, until cheese bubbles and turns golden.

Serves 4

Per serving:

Calories: 301
Fat: 5 g

Veal-y Delicious Picatta with Capers

With its sharp, fresh taste thanks to the lemons and pickled capers, veal picatta is a main course that also looks lovely on a serving platter, surrounded by thin slices of lemon. If you prefer, boneless, skinless chicken breasts pounded between waxed paper to 1/4-inch (1cm) thickness can be substituted for veal.

> 1/2 tbsp (7 mL) olive oil
> 4 veal cutlets, pounded 1/4-inch (1 cm) thick
> 1 clove garlic, minced
> 2 tbsp (30 mL) fresh lemon juice
> 1/4 cup (50 mL) dry white wine
> 2 tsp (10 mL) capers, drained and rinsed
> salt and pepper to taste
> lemon slices for garnish

Heat 1 teaspoon (5 mL) of the olive oil in a large non-stick skillet. Add the veal cutlets and cook over medium-high heat for about 2 minutes per side until nicely browned. Transfer veal to a plate and keep warm.

Add the remaining oil to the pan and add the garlic. Sauté for 1 minute over medium heat. Don't let the garlic brown, or it will be bitter. Add the lemon juice, wine, capers, salt and pepper and cook for 1 minute. Put the veal back into the skillet and reheat 1 to 2 minutes. Transfer to a serving platter and garnish with the lemon slices.

Venus Sorbet

Serves 4

Per serving

Calories: 117
Fat: I g

According to Roman mythology, Venus was the goddess of love and beauty. She's the inspiration for this luscious, sensual, nectarine sorbet. Smooth, silky and just a bit decadent. It's easy to double the recipe, too, for those times you're entertaining on a grand scale.

> 4 ripe nectarines, peeled and pitted
> 1 cup (250 mL) orange juice
> 1/4 cup (50 mL) low-fat vanilla yogurt
> 2 tbsp (30 mL) granulated sugar
> 4 small mint sprigs for garnish

In a food processor or blender, combine nectarines, juice, yogurt and sugar. Process until smooth. Pour mixture into a 9-inch (22 cm) cake pan. Cover and freeze for 4 hours or until firm.

Before serving, let it soften slightly at room temperature. Spoon sorbet into a bowl or wine goblet and garnish with a mint sprig.

Apricot Biscotti

These crispy, crunchy, twice-baked biscuits are perfect for dipping in your after-dinner cappuccino (made with skim milk, of course).

> 3 cups (750 mL) all-purpose flour
> 1 tsp (5 mL) baking powder
> pinch of salt
> 1/4 cup (50 mL) margarine, at room temperature
> 2/3 cup (170 mL) granulated sugar
> egg substitute (equivalent to 3 eggs)
> 1 tbsp (15 mL) grated lemon zest
> 1 tbsp (15 mL) lemon juice
> 3/4 tsp (5 mL) anise extract or almond extract
> 1 1/4 cups (300 mL) chopped dried apricots

Preheat oven to 350°F (180°C). In a bowl, combine the flour, baking powder and salt.

In another bowl, cream together the margarine and sugar. Beat in the egg substitute a little at a time. Add the lemon zest, juice and anise extract and mix well. Add the dry ingredients to the wet mixture a little at a time, beating until almost combined. Add the dried apricots and beat until combined.

Divide the dough in half and shape into 2 loaves 2 1/2 inches (6.25 cm) wide. Place them on a non-stick baking sheet and bake for 30 minutes until lightly browned. Transfer to a rack and cool completely.

With a serrated knife, cut each loaf into slices 3/8-inch (8 mm) thick on the diagonal. Place slices back on the cookie sheet and broil 5 inches (12 cm) from heat source for 1 minute per side until golden brown. Let cool and store in an airtight container.

Chapter 8

Grey Cup/Super Bowl Spread

Menu

Touchdown Tortilla Chips
Amazing Potato Chips
Herbed Cheese Football
Quarterback Chicken Strips
Plum Sauce
Through the Uprights Salad
Hot and Hearty Beef Stew
Skinny Spicy Fries
Chill Out Chili
Classic Creamy Coleslaw
Your Basic Pizza Dough
First Down Roasted Garlic and Tomato Pizza
Second Down Spinach and Mushroom Pizza
Long Pass Date Cookies
Wendy s 50-Yard Line Apple Crisp

Introduction

Barb loves football. Wendy doesn't know a kicker from a picker. But neither one of them would miss out on throwing, or hosting, an annual football bash.

Whether you support the CFL, NFL, English football or would rather watch paint dry, there's no better way to spend the Sunday of the big game than with a bunch of friends or family, a huge spread of fabulous food, a big TV and lots of fun and laughter.

Barb says rooting for her beloved Hamilton Tiger Cats and her long-suffering Buffalo Bills helps make fall exciting. Not to mention the thrill of winning the football pool. And the Super Bowl party she goes to each year has taught her the number-one thing needed to make this kind of bash a hit: two TVs. Put one in the kitchen, so that the party can spill in there and still let people follow the game no matter where they like to hang out. Makes the guys spend some time in the kitchen with the girls, too, which always adds to the fun, not to mention the kitchen duty staff!

As for Wendy, Grey Cup and Super Bowl Sundays are less about the game and more about female bonding. It lets the gals kick back and be loud, whether they follow the action on the field or not.

And, of course, it's also about food. Football eats should be hearty, things that go well on a buffet table, or in a picnic basket for a tailgate party. We thought of rib-sticking recipes, and also great snacking fare. After all, what's a primo game of football without a big bowl of chips and dip? We can't imagine watching the action without 'em. The trick is to keep the fat and calories down, and we've done just that. Amazing Potato Chips, Touchdown Tortilla

Chips (both with dips), pizza with fantastic low-fat toppings, Hot and Hearty Beef Stew, all followed up with a bowl of Wendy's awesome 50-Yard Line Apple Crisp.

Nobody will be offside when they dig into this spread. Now, if the TiCats could only win the Grey Cup, life would be perfect.

Y Cocktails

When it comes to football, the drink is beer.

You can make cocktails for a Grey Cup or Super Bowl bash and even incorporate the colors of the two teams, say a ruby red Seabreeze for the Phoenix Cardinals, or a bright orange Screwdriver for the Tiger Cats. But when you get down to it, most football partiers want nothing more than a frosty mug of brew.

Here are our suggestions for some brands you might want to try:

Rickard's Red (Canada)
Creemore Lager (Canada)
Molson Black Horse (Canada)
Kokanee (Canada)
Sol (Mexico)
Samuel Adams (United States)
Kirin (Japan)

Music Picks

Provided you can hear the music over the TV!

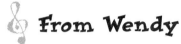 **From Wendy**

The Eagles, *Hell Freezes Over.* Geffen.

From Barb

Rolling Stones. *Hot Rocks*. AbKco.

Touchdown Tortilla Chips

Oh-so-easy to make, and guaranteed to make you a first-round draft pick with the gang.

8 10-inch (25 cm) flour tortillas

Preheat oven to 350°F (180°C). Cut each tortilla into 12 wedges. Lay them flat in a single layer on a baking sheet and bake for about 8 minutes, or until they start to brown. Cool on a rack. The chips will crisp up as they cool. Repeat with remaining wedges.

Serve the tortilla chips with Wendy and Barb's "You Won't Believe This Is Low-Fat" Skinny Dips like Hummus, Baba-ghanouj and Bruschetta.

Wendy and Barb's Kitchen Staples

Keep these handy and you'll always have a low-fat meal or snack just minutes away.

- **Canned white beans. Perfect to purée as a dip, bread spread, or to thicken soups and stews.**
- **Low-fat cottage cheese.**
- **Pizza shells or tortillas.** Top with sauce, a sprinkle of oregano and basil, sliced veggies, capers, low-fat cheese and pop in the oven for an instant pizza fix.
- **Pasta... a million kinds to try, all fat-free.**
- **Tuna packed in water.** Dolphin friendly, 'cause we love Flipper. Whip up a light tuna salad, mix with pasta or put in a low-fat casserole.
- **Boneless, skinless chicken breasts.** The basis for a ton of great meals. Save some money and bone them yourselves. It's so easy, even we can do it.
- **Salsa.** Use as a base for salad dressing, dip baked tortilla chips in it, cook chicken in it, toss with pasta. It's great stuff.
- **Fruit.** Purée berries to top low-fat ice cream or stir into yogurt. Buzz frozen fruits in the blender with sweetener for a luscious fruit ice.
- **Frozen veggies.** Add to chicken stock for a quick soup, toss with pasta.

Amazing Potato Chips

Serves 20

Per serving
(20 chips):

Calories: 115
Fat: 3 g

It is every person's right to be able to grab a handful of potato chips and munch out when watching sporting events. And you're no exception. In fact, you get two handfuls. And it's all legal. Amazing, isn't it?

> 10 large baking potatoes, washed
> 2 tsp (10 mL) olive oil
> salt to taste

Preheat oven to 350°F (180°C). Slice the potatoes as thinly as possible, no thicker than 1/8 inch (2 mm). Pat potatoes dry.

Spray a non-stick baking sheet with a light coating of cooking spray. Arrange potato slices in a single layer on the sheet and brush a little of the oil on each. Sprinkle with salt.

Bake for 15 to 20 minutes until lightly browned. Remove and cool.

The Skinny on Candy

Here's some sweet news. Hard candies and jelly beans have absolutely no fat although, be warned, they are loaded with sugar. When an overwhelming sweet craving hits, try a few jelly beans or a couple of Life Savers. It's better than pigging out on a chocolate bar. And don't forget Wendy and Barb's secret weapon: pre-sweetened cereals like Froot Loops or Frosted Flakes. One cup (250 mL) of Cap'n Crunch has just 120 calories and 1.6 grams of fat. Munch a sweet handful from the box and banish cravings.

Herbed Cheese Football

A wooden platter with a cheese ball sitting in the middle is a party staple, but you can avoid the heart-attack-on-a-plate syndrome with our yummy light version. And if you're feeling like having fun, why not shape it into a football? The directions are below.

> **1 8-oz (250 g) package farmer's cheese**
> **1/2 cup (125 mL) 1% cottage cheese**
> **1/2 cup (125 mL) shredded low-fat cheddar**
>   **cheese**
> **1 tbsp (15 mL) minced fresh rosemary**
> **1/2 tsp (2 mL) dry mustard**
> **1/8 tsp (0.5 mL) pepper**
> **1/3 cup (75 mL) minced fresh parsley**
> **bunch of fresh chives, left whole (optional)**

In a food processor, whirl the 3 cheeses, rosemary, mustard and pepper for 30 seconds. No food processor? No problem. Just grab a potato masher or a fork and mash all ingredients until they're combined. On a sheet of plastic wrap, shape the mixture into a log. Wrap tightly and refrigerate overnight. To serve, remove the plastic wrap. Sprinkle the parsley on a piece of waxed paper and roll the log in the parsley, pressing to help it adhere. Or, before refrigerating, shape the cheese into a football shape instead of a log. When you unwrap it, skip the parsley and instead use the chives to make seams and laces on the "football." Sure, it's corny, but it's also fun.

Serve with an assortment of low-fat crackers, topped with roasted red pepper strips. If you're serving apple or pear wedges, sprinkle fruit with lemon juice so they don't discolor.

Quarterback Chicken Strips

Serves 4

Per serving:

Calories: 300
Fat: 4 g

Chicken fingers are always a big score, but when they're deep-fried, your pass towards health is definitely intercepted. Try making them our way, with none of the fat and all the extra-crunchy great taste. Little football fans love these but you may want to skip the cayenne for them. Stick around for the plum sauce recipe. It's up next.

> 1/2 cup (125 mL) skim milk
> 1/2 tsp (2 mL) honey
> 1 1/2 cups (375 mL) crushed corn flakes
> 1/4 tsp (1 mL) salt
> 1/4 tsp (1 mL) black pepper
> 1/4 tsp (1 mL) cayenne pepper
> 1 lb (500 g) boneless, skinless chicken breasts, cut
>   in strips

Preheat the oven to 400°F (200°C).

Spray a non-stick baking sheet with cooking spray. In a bowl, combine the milk and honey, and set aside. You may find the honey mixes a bit better if you melt it in the microwave for a few seconds first. On a plate, combine the corn flakes, salt, pepper and cayenne. Put the chicken strips in the milk mixture and toss to coat. Place one strip at a time on the plate with the corn flake crumbs and roll it until coated, pressing lightly to help them flakes stick. Place on the baking sheet and repeat with remaining strips. Bake for 8 to 10 minutes until cooked through, crisp and golden brown. Place on serving platter and pass the plum sauce.

Makes ¹/₂ cup (125 mL)

Per serving (1 tbsp/15 mL):

Calories: 16
Fat: 0 g

Plum Sauce

1/2 cup (125 mL) bottled plum sauce
1 tsp (5 mL) finely grated lemon zest
1 tbsp (15 mL) lemon juice
1 tsp (5 mL) soy sauce or teriyaki sauce

Mix all ingredients in a small bowl until well combined. Refrigerate until ready to serve. Serve as a dipping sauce with the Quarterback Chicken Strips.

Through the Uprights Salad

Serves 6
Per serving:
Calories: 65
Fat: 1.5 g

Here's jicama again, that crunchy, mild veggie you met in our Olé Mexican Spread in Chapter 6. Wendy's sister Lori says once you try jicama, you'll love it. She even likes to peel it, cut it into sticks and eat it with dip. Check it out.

> 3 cups (750 mL) jicama, diced
> 2 cups (500 mL) cucumbers, seeded, unpeeled
>   and diced
> 1 cup (250 mL) radishes, cut in half and sliced
> 3 tbsp (45 mL) chopped fresh parsley
> 2 tsp (10 mL) olive oil
> 2 tbsp (30 mL) fresh lime juice
> salt and pepper to taste

Mix jicama, cucumber and radish in a bowl. Whisk together the parsley, oil, lime juice, salt and pepper. Pour over vegetables and toss. Refrigerate until ready to serve.

Hot and Hearty Beef Stew

This is the good stuff, a rich stew chock full of tender meat, vegetables and spices, all simmered in our special secret sauce. The secret? Well, there are two. The first is, this is a skinny stew with just 5 grams of fat per serving. The second is the bottle of beer that makes the beef melt in your mouth and taste like it's been cooking all day. But you can have this dish on the table in 30 minutes.

> 1 lb (500 g) beef top round, cut in 1-inch (2 cm) cubes
> 1 tsp (5 mL) olive oil
> 2 onions, cut in half and sliced
> 4 cloves garlic, minced
> 2 carrots, sliced
> 1 bottle of beer
> 1 cup (250 mL) frozen peas
> 1 cup (250 mL) vegetable broth
> 1 tbsp (15 mL) Worcestershire or H.P. sauce
> 1/2 tsp (2 mL) marjoram
> 1/2 tsp (2 mL) red pepper flakes
> salt and pepper to taste
> 1 tbsp (15 mL) Bisto
> 2 tbsp (30 mL) cold water
> 1/4 cup (50 mL) chopped fresh parsley

In a large non-stick saucepan, heat the oil. Add the beef and cook, stirring constantly, just until browned on all sides. Remove the beef to a plate and keep warm.

Add the onions, garlic and carrots to the pan and sauté for about 5 minutes. Add the beer, and cook over high heat for about 3 minutes until alcohol has evaporated. Add the peas, broth, Worcestershire, marjoram and red pepper flakes. Bring to a boil and reduce heat. Simmer for 10 minutes. Season with salt and pepper. In a small bowl, mix the Bisto and cold water into a smooth mixture. Add to the pan, stirring constantly until stew thickens slightly, about 2 minutes. Return beef to pan. Ladle stew into bowls and garnish with chopped parsley.

Serves 4

Per serving:

Calories: 136
Fat: 3 g

Skinny Spicy Fries

Oven fries are a delicious alternative to the deep-fried guys. We've added some extra interest with Italian spice.

> 1 1/2 lb (750 g) large baking potatoes, scrubbed
> 1/3 cup (75 mL) low- or non-fat Italian dressing
> 1/3 cup (75 mL) Parmesan cheese
> 1/2 tsp (2 mL) dried oregano
> 1/4 tsp (1 mL) dried rosemary
> salt and pepper to taste

Preheat oven to 400°F (200°C). Cut the potatoes in half lengthwise, then in half crosswise. Cut each quarter into 3 to 4 wedges.

Put the dressing, Parmesan, oregano, rosemary, salt and pepper in a large plastic bag. Seal the bag, put on some hot tunes and shake, shake, shake to mix. Add the potatoes in batches and keep up that shaking action. Arrange potato wedges in a single layer on a non-stick baking sheet (you may need two sheets).

Bake for 40 to 50 minutes, turning occasionally, until tender and golden brown.

174 ◇ Spread Yourself Thin

Chill-Out Chili

It's always a good idea to have one vegetarian dish on any buffet. Here's a delicious chili with lots of kick that uses no meat. The heady aroma that invades your kitchen when you whip up this quick chili is guaranteed to have them holding out their bowls and begging, even the beef eaters in your bunch.

1 tbsp (15 mL) margarine
4 onions, chopped
4 cloves garlic, minced
2 tbsp (30 mL) chili powder
2 tsp (10 mL) cumin
1/4 tsp (1 mL) allspice
1/2 tsp (2 mL) salt
1/2 tsp (2 mL) black pepper
1/4 tsp (1 mL) cayenne pepper
2 red peppers, diced
2 green peppers diced
2 yellow peppers, diced
1 jalapeño, seeded and minced (wear gloves for this)
2 large carrots, shredded
1 28-oz (796 mL) can diced tomatoes, with liquid
1 7 1/2-oz (213 mL) can tomato sauce
1 4-oz (114 mL) can tomato paste
2 cups (500 mL) vegetable broth
1 19-oz (540 mL) can red kidney beans
1 19-oz (540 mL) can pinto beans
1/2 cup (125 mL) fresh chopped coriander or parsley

In a large non-stick saucepan, heat the margarine over medium high heat. Add the onions, garlic and seasonings and sauté for 4 to 5 minutes until the onions start to soften. Add the peppers, jalapeño and carrots and sauté 5 minutes more. Add the tomatoes, sauce, paste and broth and simmer for 30 minutes, stirring occasionally.

Stir in the beans and coriander. Cook for about 10 minutes more or until the beans are heated through.

The Skinny on Spices that Can Make You Slim

There is some evidence that using certain spices does a lot more than liven up your food. Some may even help you lose weight. Among the top choices — garlic, chili powder, parsley, fennel seed, ginger and celery seed.

Classic Creamy Coleslaw

Serves 8

Per serving:

Calories: 49
Fat: 1 g

Red onion looks great with Green cabbage and this slightly sweet-yet-sour, creamy dressing is pure classic coleslaw, but without the fat. You'll score a touchdown with this one.

> 6 cups (1.5 L) thinly shredded green cabbage
> 1 red onion, thinly sliced
> 1 tbsp (15 mL) chopped fresh dill
> 2 tbsp (30 mL) chopped fresh parsley
> 1/2 cup (125 mL) non-fat sour cream
> 1/2 cup (125 mL) red wine vinegar
> 2 1/2 tsp (12 mL) granulated sugar
> salt and pepper to taste

Mix the cabbage, onion, dill and parsley in a large bowl. In a small bowl, mix together the sour cream, vinegar, sugar, salt and pepper. Pour dressing over the cabbage mixture and toss to combine.

Serves 4

Per serving:

Calories: 383
Fat: 1.3 g

Your Basic Pizza Dough

Have to have pizza when the game is on. Why hope the delivery guy makes it before the first play when *you* can, and it's all low-fat, sizzling and mouth-watering, straight from your oven?

> 1 cup (250 mL) warm water
> 1 package (8 g) active dry yeast
> 1/8 tsp (0.5 mL) salt
> 2 cups (500 mL) all-purpose flour
> 1 1/2 cups (375 mL) whole wheat flour

In a large bowl, measure out the water, yeast and salt. Stir to combine and set aside until mixture becomes foamy, about 5 minutes.

Stir the all-purpose flour into the yeast mixture until smooth. Add 1 1/4 cups (300 mL) whole wheat flour and mix. Add enough remaining whole wheat flour to form a soft dough. Turn the dough out onto a floured board and knead until smooth and elastic, about 6 minutes. Pretend it's the quarterback of the opposing team!

Place dough in a very lightly oiled bowl, cover and set in a warm place to rise until doubled in bulk, about 2 hours.

Punch down the dough and turn out onto a board. Knead for 2 minutes. Return dough to bowl, cover and let rise 1 more hour.

At this point, the dough is ready to be rolled out and spread with your favorite topping. This recipe makes enough for one 12-inch (30 cm) thick crust pizza or, if you prefer a thinner crust, roll dough out and place on two smaller, lightly sprayed baking sheets.

First Down Roasted Garlic and Tomato Pizza

Serves 4

Per serving

Calories: 390
Fat: 2.3 g

1 pizza crust, pre-baked
1 head roasted garlic
2 plum tomatoes, thinly sliced
2 tbsp (30 mL) chopped fresh basil
2 tsp (10 mL) olive oil

To prepare pizza crust:
Prepare pizza dough as directed on previous page. Bake in a preheated 450°F (230° C) oven for about 5 minutes, or until browned and crisp.

To roast garlic:
Preheat oven to 350°F (180°C). With a sharp knife, cut the top 1/8" of the garlic head off and discard. Wrap whole head in a double thickness of aluminum foil and bake for 45 to 60 minutes, or until the cloves are very soft. Squeeze cloves out of skins into a small bowl and mash with a fork.

Spread prepared pizza crust with the roasted garlic. Arrange the tomato slices over the top in an attractive pattern. Sprinkle with basil and drizzle the oil over the top. Bake just until heated through and tomatoes start to wilt, about 10 to 15 minutes.

Serves 4

Per serving:

Calories: 392
Fat: 2.7 g

Second Down Spinach and Mushroom Pizza

1 unbaked pizza crust
1 tsp (5 mL) olive oil
1 onion, finely chopped
5 oz (140 g) mushrooms, thinly sliced
salt and pepper to taste
2 10-oz (284 g) packages frozen spinach, chopped
   and squeezed dry
2 cloves garlic, minced
1/2 cup (125 mL) low-fat mozzarella, shredded
1/4 cup (50 mL) chopped fresh basil or parsley

Preheat oven to 450°F (230°C). In a non-stick skillet, heat the oil over medium heat and add the onion. Sauté, stirring occasionally, for about 5 minutes. Add the mushrooms, salt and pepper and sauté for another 3 minutes. Add the spinach and garlic and cook, stirring, about 3 more minutes until mixture is fairly dry.

Spread the spinach mixture over the pizza dough. Sprinkle with the mozzarella and basil. Bake for 10 to 15 minutes or until edges of crust are nicely browned.

Just a Suggestion

Any of the low-fat pestos from the Mama Mia Spread in Chapter 7 make excellent pizza toppings. Just spread the one of your choice over an unbaked pizza crust and top it with roasted or raw veggies; canned, drained artichoke hearts, chopped; seafood; or just a little low-fat shredded cheese. Use your imagination and come up with your own skinny signature pizza! For a party, why not let the gang custom-design their own pizzas from a bar of assorted toppings?

Long Pass Date Cookies

Makes 30 cookies

Per cookie:

Calories: 71
Fat 2 g

Rich and chewy, date cookies are always satisfying. We took fat out of the game and sent in flavor to make the play.

1/3 cup (75 mL) soft margarine
2/3 cup (150 mL) packed brown sugar
1 egg, lightly beaten
1 tbsp (15 mL) grated lemon zest
3/4 cup (175 mL) all-purpose flour
2/3 cup (150 mL) whole wheat flour
1 1/2 tsp (7 mL) baking powder
1/2 tsp (2 mL) cinnamon
1/2 tsp (2 mL) nutmeg
1 cup (250 mL) dates, chopped
1/4 cup (50 mL) skim milk

Preheat oven to 325°F (160°C).

In a large bowl, cream the margarine and sugar together until light and creamy. Beat in egg and lemon zest. In a second bowl, combine the flours, baking powder, cinnamon and nutmeg and mix well. Stir in the chopped dates. Alternately add the dry ingredients and milk to the wet mixture, stirring well after each addition.

Drop by spoonfuls onto a non-stick cookie sheet and bake for 13 to 15 minutes. Remove to a wire rack to cool.

Serves 6

Per serving:

Calories: 184
Fat: 1.2 g

Wendy's 50-Yard Line Apple Crisp

Inviting, aromatic apple crisp. A fall classic. Warm apples cooked to comfort-food softness with cinnamon and nutmeg, all nestled below a crunchy-sweet oat topping with just a hint of orange. Use any apples you fancy, Granny Smith, Spy, Spartan, and don't forget that made-in-Canada superstar, the Macintosh.

> 4 cups (1 L) sliced apples
> 1/4 cup (50 mL) raisins
> 3/4 cup (175 mL) quick-cooking oats
> 3 tbsp (45 mL) all-purpose flour
> 1/4 cup (50 mL) brown sugar
> 1/2 tsp (2 mL) cinnamon
> 1/4 tsp (1 mL) nutmeg
> 1 tbsp (15 mL) soft margarine
> 2 to 3 tbsp (30 to 45 mL) orange juice

Preheat oven to 375°F (190°C).

In a bowl, combine the apples and raisins.

Coat a 9-inch (22 cm) baking pan with cooking spray. Spread the apples out evenly in pan.

In a large bowl, stir together the oats, flour, sugar, cinnamon and nutmeg until combined. Work in the margarine until mixture is crumbly, adding a little orange juice at a time to help this process. Sprinkle topping over apples. Bake for about 30 minutes.

Serve with low-fat frozen vanilla yogurt.

The Skinny on Wendy's Crisp

You can substitute any fruit of your choice for apples. How about a combination of apple and rhubarb, apple-blackberry or fresh or frozen peaches?

The Skinny on Substitutions

Don't give up all your favorites, just change them to cut fat and calories. Most recipes will adapt well, although Grandma's deep-fried chocolate fudge may pose a problem. You'll have to experiment to find what works in recipes. When making sweet stuff, cut butter back and replace it with jam, jelly or honey. If you must, use margarine, but sparingly. Remember it's 100% fat! Use non-stick spray instead of oil in your frying pan. Sauté in broth or wine. Use low-fat sour cream, low-fat yogurt or evaporated skim milk instead of fatty, creamy stuff. Cut back on full-fat cheeses and use skim milk varieties.

The Skinny on Chocolate Chip Cookies

When you feel like raiding the fridge, here's a delicious treat.

Wendy and Barb's Choco-lotto Crisps

1 cup (250 mL) all-purpose flour
1/2 tsp (2 mL) baking soda
1/2 tsp (2 mL) salt
2 tbsp (30 mL) butter
2 oz (55 g) reduced-fat cream cheese
6 tbsp (90 mL) packed brown sugar
6 tbsp (90 mL) white sugar
1 egg
1 egg white
1/2 cup (125 mL) chocolate chips, coarsely chopped

Preheat oven to 375°F (190°C).

Spray two cookie sheets with cooking spray and set aside.

In a small bowl, stir together flour, baking soda and salt. Set aside. Melt the butter over low heat. Cook about 1 minute, until butter browns slightly. Don't let it burn. Pour into a mixing bowl and add cream cheese and sugars. Beat with an electric mixer on low speed until smooth. Add the egg and egg white, beating well. Add the dry ingredients and chocolate chips and mix until combined. Do not overmix.

Drop batter by tablespoonfuls, 2 inches (5 cm) apart on the cookie sheets. Bake 1 sheet at a time for 12 to 15 minutes. Let cool on racks.

Makes about 30 cookies
Per cookie:
Calories: 63
Fat: 2 g

Chapter 9

Thanksgiving Spread

Menu

Slim and Sassy Spinach Dip with Mint
Crab and Artichoke Tartlets
Creamy Dream of Broccoli Soup
Fancy Greens with Pine Nuts and Balsamic Dressing
Classic Roast Turkey
Go Wild Rice Stuffing
Savory Onion and Mushroom Stuffing
Rich Turkey Gravy
Cranberry-Orange Relish to Relish
Buttermilk Mashed Potatoes
Sweet Potato Casserole
Gobble Gobble Stuffed Squash
Roasted Vegetables with Fresh Sage
Sweet and Aromatic Pumpkin Bread Pudding
Suave Poached Pears with Blackberry Sauce

Introduction

Thanksgiving seems to find many of us settling into the blocks, awaiting the starter's pistol for that great marathon of non-stop holiday eating. Bang. We're off. The next sound you hear will be "Happy New Year" and your zipper bursting.

We decided that we didn't want to live that way anymore. Wouldn't it be better, we figured, to be able to sit down with friends and family for a big Thanksgiving spread that didn't leave us feeling bloated, sluggish and, worst of all, guilty?

Thanksgiving always means new beginnings to Wendy because her birthday falls in October. It always feels like New Year's, but instead of January's snows, there are the sights and sounds of harvest time, fall colors and that first chill in the air marking a fresh start. Let this spread signify a new beginning for you, too, as you host a traditional holiday in a healthy way, maybe for the first time ever.

Looking for a way to make sure the day is just as much fun for the cook as the guests? Barb always roasts her turkey the day before. Make sure you remove all the stuffing, carve the cooked bird, toss the carcass (or freeze to make soup later) and store the meat and dressing in the refrigerator the night before. Put the chilled main course, covered, in the oven to reheat before dinner. Trust me, Barb says, the kitchen smells just as good as if you were actually roasting Tom, and there's no big carving mess on the table.

To prove eating smart doesn't mean deprivation, we have included all your classic favorite Thanksgiving foods in our spread, a golden-roasted turkey (with your choice of two dressings) with all the trimmings, from cranberry-orange relish to rich-tasting gravy. Since Thanksgiving is about traditions for many of us, we've tried to include the kinds of foods that evoke warm memories. Did Grandma always make a sweet potato casserole? It's here. Wouldn't dream of starting without a cream soup from Aunt Millie's heirloom tureen? We've got it — Creamy Dream of Broccoli Soup. And just to keep things interesting, we've added modern classics like Fancy Greens with Pine Nuts and Balsamic Dressing and Sweet and Aromatic Pumpkin Bread Pudding.

We have a lot to be thankful for — family, pals, a successful business, our friendship and lean, healthy bodies that stopped being the enemy a long time ago. We wish all these things for you, too. Happy Thanksgiving!

Cocktails
Spiced Cider

When you first feel that snap of fall in the air, it's time to build the first fire of the season and snuggle up with a steaming glass of fragrant spiced cider. This recipe doubles or triples easily to serve a crowd. Kids love it, and enjoy having a hot drink with the big people. Ladle it from a crockpot to keep the mixture warm between servings.

> 4 cups (1 L) apple cider
> 1 cinnamon stick
> 1 lemon slice
> 1 orange slice, the rind studded with:
> 4 whole cloves
> 2 slices fresh ginger, about 1/4-inch (1 cm) thick
> cinnamon sticks to garnish

In a saucepan over high heat, combine all the ingredients except cinnamon stick garnishes. Bring to a boil, cover the pan, and remove from heat. Let stand 15 minutes to allow flavors to combine. Strain and pour into 4 mugs or a crockpot to serve a crowd. Garnish each mug with a cinnamon stick.

Wine Suggestions
Cabernet Sauvignon or Sauvignon Blanc

Music Picks

 ## From Wendy

Itzhak Perlman, Daniel Barenboim, *The Three Violins*. Sony.

From Barb

Tony Bennett, *On Holiday.* Columbia.

Makes 1½ cups
(375 mL)

Per serving
(1 tbsp/15 mL):

Calories: 15
Fat: 0 g

Slim and Sassy
Spinach Dip with Mint

You know that yummy spinach dip that somebody always brings to parties that tastes so good, but it's just jammed with mayo and sour cream? Well, here's our version. You'll be thankful that it contains big taste and absolutely no fat.

1 1/4 cups (300 mL) non-fat sour cream
1/2 cup (125 mL) chopped frozen spinach,
   squeezed dry
1/4 cup (50 mL) chopped fresh mint
1 green onion, chopped
1 garlic clove, minced
1/4 tsp (1 mL) grated lemon zest
1/4 tsp (1 mL) salt
few drops hot pepper sauce

Put all the ingredients in a food processor or blender and purée until smooth. You can also just mix all the ingredients in a bowl for a dip with a little more texture. Refrigerate until ready to serve. Serve with raw vegetables, low-fat crackers or mini-pitas.

The Skinny on a Happening Buffet

Here's a great tip: Stack the plates at the start of your buffet table and the silverware at the end. No more balancing plates and cutlery. Neat trick.

Crab and Artichoke Tartlets

Makes 28 tartlets

Per tartlet:

Calories: 35
Fat: 0.7 g

Crab and artichokes make a delectable combination, especially served up in savory custard and nestled in crispy, thin shells.

> 1 4-oz (114 mL) carton egg substitute
> 2 tbsp (30 mL) all-purpose flour
> 1/8 tsp (0.5 mL) dried thyme
> 1/8 tsp (0.5 mL) pepper
> 1/4 cup (50 mL) roasted red peppers, chopped (drained and patted dry on paper towels if using jarred variety packed in oil)
> 1 14-oz (398 mL) can artichokes, drained and chopped
> 1 4.2-oz (120 g) can crabmeat, drained, picked over, and flaked
> 28 wonton wrappers, measuring 3 1/4 x 3 inches (8 x 7 cm)
> 2 tbsp (30 mL) chopped chives
> 3 tbsp (45 mL) Parmesan cheese
> 1 tbsp (15 mL) soft margarine, melted

Preheat oven to 350°F (180°C).

In a bowl, combine the egg substitute, flour, thyme and pepper. Add red peppers, artichokes and crabmeat and stir to combine. Coat 28 muffin cups with cooking spray and gently press a wonton wrapper in each one. Don't worry if the edges hang over, they're supposed to. Spoon some of the crab mixture into each cup and sprinkle with a little of the chives and the Parmesan. Brush the exposed edges of the wonton wrappers with the melted margarine and bake for 20 minutes.

Serves 4

Per serving:

Calories: 102
Fat: 1.5 g

Creamy Dream of Broccoli Soup

You'll never miss the cream in this velvety soup.

1 tsp (5 mL) soft margarine
1/4 cup (50 mL) finely diced onion
2 garlic cloves, minced
2 1/2 cups (675 mL) chopped broccoli, lightly
  steamed
3 cups (750 mL) vegetable broth
2/3 cup (150 mL) skim milk powder
1/2 cup (125 mL) buttermilk
1 tbsp (15 mL) chopped fresh parsley
1 tbsp (15 mL) fresh lemon juice
1 tsp (5 mL) grated lemon zest
1 tbsp (15 mL) dry sherry
2 tbsp (30 mL) cornstarch, mixed with 1/4 cup
  (50 mL) cold water
salt and pepper to taste

Heat margarine in a non-stick saucepan and sauté the onion and garlic. Add the broccoli and sauté for 1 minute more. Add the broth, milk powder, buttermilk, parsley, lemon juice, lemon zest and sherry. Cook over low heat just until hot. Transfer to a blender or food processor and purée until smooth. Return the mixture to the saucepan and add the cornstarch mixture. Cook over low heat, stirring constantly, until thickened. Season with salt and pepper. Ladle into soup bowls or a tureen and serve.

Fancy Greens with Pine Nuts and Balsamic Dressing

We use vegetable broth to replace oil in salad dressings and it really works. Try it in place of oil in your favorite recipe or, better yet, with this classic balsamic vinaigrette.

> 6 cups (1.5 L) mixed greens
> 3/4 cup (175 mL) vegetable broth
> 1/4 cup (50 mL) balsamic vinegar
> 1 tbsp (15 mL) capers
> 2 tsp (10 mL) Dijon mustard
> 1 1/2 tsp (7 mL) dried basil
> 2 tbsp (30 mL) pine nuts

Put the greens in a large bowl. In a separate bowl, whisk together the broth, vinegar, capers, mustard and basil. Pour the dressing over the greens and toss together. Sprinkle the pine nuts over the top and serve.

The Skinny on Pine Nuts

Yes, they're high in fat, but so full of flavor, you don't need many. Always toast pine nuts in a warm oven or in a non-stick skillet for a few minutes to bring out all the flavor, but watch them carefully. Pine nuts burn very quickly.

Serves 8

5 oz (140 g) white meat, no skin:
Calories: 219
Fat: 4.5 g

5 oz (140 g) dark meat, no skin:
Calories: 262
Fat: 10 g

Classic Roast Turkey

Here it is, the main event. If you can get a free-range or never-frozen turkey from your butcher, go for it. And when it comes time to tuck into Tom, take a look at the fat and calorie comparison for white and dark meat. The dark has twice the fat of light, so choose accordingly. And skinless keeps you skinny.

> 1 16-lb (7.25 kg) turkey
> salt and pepper to taste
> 1 recipe stuffing

Preheat oven to 375°F (190°C). Remove the neck and giblets from the turkey and discard or reserve for another use. Clean out all fat from the cavity of the turkey. Rinse the cavity under running water and dry with paper towels. Season the cavity with salt and pepper. Turn the turkey breast-side up and stuff the main cavity with the stuffing of your choice (recipes follow). Put a piece of aluminum foil over the exposed stuffing and tie the drumsticks together with kitchen string.

Put the turkey breast side up on a rack in a roasting pan, and roast it in the lower half of the oven for 15 to 25 minutes per pound (30 to 50 minutes per kilogram), or until juices run clear at the thigh when pierced with a knife. If using a meat thermometer, stick the thermometer into the thickest part of the thigh not touching the bone. When the temperature reaches 180°F (80°C) the turkey is done. Remove the turkey from the oven and let it rest for 20 minutes before carving. If the turkey browns too much during cooking, cover it loosely with aluminum foil.

Go Wild Rice Stuffing

Serves 6

Per serving:

Calories: 205
Fat: 3 g

Wild rice with its chewy, nutty texture is perfect with turkey.

> 1 tsp (5 mL) soft margarine
> 1 onion, finely diced
> 3 carrots, finely diced
> 1 stalk celery, finely diced
> 1/2 tsp (2 mL) dried thyme
> 1/2 tsp (2 mL) dried rosemary
> 1 bay leaf
> 1 1/2 cups (375 mL) wild rice, rinsed well
> 2 1/2 cups (675 mL) hot vegetable broth
> salt and pepper to taste

In a non-stick skillet, heat the margarine and add the onions, carrots and celery. Sauté over medium heat for 10 minutes until vegetables are soft. Add the thyme, rosemary, bay leaf, rice and broth. Cover and simmer for about 30 minutes, stirring occasionally. When the rice is cooked, it should be tender and appear as if the grains had popped open, showing white insides. Drain off any leftover cooking liquid and season with salt and pepper. Remove the bay leaf and set the rice aside to cool slightly before stuffing the turkey. Any leftover stuffing can be cooked in a separate covered baking dish, beside the turkey, in the last 20 minutes of cooking time.

Savory Onion and Mushroom Stuffing

A traditional bread stuffing, bursting with the flavors of celery and sage. Our twist is we use bread crumbs instead of cubes. It makes for a different texture. Give it a try.

> 3 cups (750 mL) whole wheat bread crumbs
> 1 1/2 cups (375 mL) mushrooms, cleaned and chopped
> 1 cup (250 mL) celery with leaves, finely chopped
> 2 onions, finely chopped
> 1 tsp (5 mL) dried thyme
> 1 tsp (5 mL) dried rosemary
> 1 tsp (5 mL) dried sage
> 2 tbsp (30 mL) chopped fresh parsley
> salt and pepper to taste
> 1/4 cup (50 mL) vegetable broth

In a large bowl, combine the bread crumbs, mushrooms, celery, onions, thyme, rosemary, sage, parsley, salt and pepper. Stir to combine ingredients. Sprinkle broth over and mix until mixture is just slightly moistened. Fill cavity of turkey with stuffing.

Rich Turkey Gravy

Serves 8

Per serving
(1/3 cup/80 mL):

Calories: 32
Fat: 1 g

Don't be a turkey. You've gotta have gravy. And ours is rich, delicious and legal.

> defatted turkey drippings
> 1/4 cup (50 mL) minced onion
> 1/4 tsp (1 mL) celery seed
> 2 tbsp (30 mL) all-purpose flour
> 2 cups (500 mL) vegetable broth
> 1 bay leaf
> 1/4 cup (50 mL) skim milk
> salt and pepper to taste

In a non-stick saucepan, heat the drippings over medium heat. Add the onion and celery seed and sauté for 5 minutes, stirring occasionally. Lower the heat and stir in the flour. Cook for 3 minutes, stirring until flour is golden in color. Stir in the broth and the bay leaf and bring to a boil. Lower the heat and simmer for 10 minutes. Add the milk, salt and pepper and simmer for 2 more minutes. Remove the bay leaf and pour gravy into a gravy boat.

Makes 1 cup
(250 mL)

Per serving
(2 tbsp/30 mL):

Calories: 25
Fat: 0 g

Cranberry-Orange Relish to Relish

There are always those who simply can't eat turkey without their cranberries. It would be like Wendy without Barb. So we came up with this slightly sweet and tart relish for you.

> 2 cups (500 mL) cranberry juice
> 1/4 cup (50 mL) orange marmalade
> 1 cup (250 mL) fresh cranberries
> 2 tbsp (30 mL) raspberry vinegar

In a saucepan over high heat, bring the cranberry juice, marmalade and cranberries to a boil. Reduce heat to medium and simmer until juice is reduced by half and cranberries are soft, about 10 minutes. Add the vinegar and simmer for 5 minutes more until sauce thickens.

Buttermilk Mashed Potatoes

Serves 4

Per serving:

Calories: 158
Fat: trace

Buttermilk adds a creamy smoothness to mashed potatoes, but without the fat. And warming the buttermilk first makes these taters heavenly.

> **2 lb (1 kg) potatoes, peeled and cut in half**
> **1/2 cup (125 mL) buttermilk**
> **salt and pepper to taste**
> **1 tbsp (15 mL) chopped fresh chives**

Put the potatoes in a large pot with enough cold water to cover. Bring to a boil, reduce heat and cook for 20 to 30 minutes, or until tender.

In a small saucepan, warm the buttermilk. Don't let it boil!

Drain and mash the potatoes in a large bowl or the pot you cooked them in. Add the buttermilk and mix well. Season with salt and pepper and stir in the chives.

Sweet Potato Casserole

We love the way apples add to this definitive dish. It's destined to be a new holiday classic on your table.

> 1 1/2 lb (750 g) sweet potatoes, peeled and cut into chunks
> 2 large baking apples, cored and cut in wedges
> 1 tsp (5 mL) cinnamon
> 1/2 tsp (2 mL) nutmeg
> 1/2 cup (125 mL) packed brown sugar
> 1/2 cup (125 mL) orange juice
> 1 tbsp (15 mL) melted soft margarine

Preheat oven to 400°F (200°C).

Place the sweet potatoes and apples in a 9-inch (22 cm) square baking dish coated with cooking spray. Sprinkle with the cinnamon, nutmeg and sugar, and toss to coat. Pour on the orange juice and melted margarine and cover with aluminum foil. Bake for 1 hour, until potatoes are tender.

Clockwise from top:
Herbed Cheese Football (p. 168)
Chill Out Chili (p. 175)
Quarterback Chicken Strips (p. 169)
Plum Sauce (p. 170)
Wendy's 50-Yard Line Apple Crisp (p. 182)
First Down Roasted Garlic and Tomato Pizza (p. 179)
"You Won't Believe This Is Low-Fat" dips:
Baba Ghanouj, Hummus and Bruschetta
Touchdown Tortilla Chips (p. 166)

Gobble Gobble Stuffed Squash

So good, your guests will gobble them up.

4 acorn squash
1 1/2 tsp (7 mL) olive oil
2 onions, chopped finely
3 stalks of celery, plus leaves, chopped finely
4 cloves of garlic, minced
2 apples, cored and diced
1 1/4 cups (300 mL) coarse bread crumbs
1 tbsp (15 mL) chopped fresh parsley
1 tbsp (15 mL) each thyme, tarragon, sage and basil
1 cup vegetable broth
1/2 cup (125 mL) raisins

Preheat oven to 350°F (180°C). Cut the squash in half, remove seeds and place on a baking sheet that has been lightly sprayed with cooking spray. Bake for 40 minutes until tender and remove from oven.

Heat the oil in a large skillet over medium heat and add the onions, celery and garlic. Sauté for 3 to 4 minutes. Add the apples and cook for another 3 minutes. Transfer mixture to a large bowl and add the bread crumbs, herbs, broth and raisins. Stir just until moistened. Season with salt and pepper and mix again. Stuff the squashes with the apple mixture and bake in a 375°F (190°C) oven for 15 to 20 minutes.

Clockwise from top:
Steve's Beef Tenderloin on Herb Biscuits with Horseradish Sauce (p. 215)
Luscious Maritime Crab Bisque (p. 211)
Summer Fruit-Spinach Salad with Raspberry Vinaigrette (p. 213)
Holiday Smoked Trout with Lime Mayonnaise (p. 214)
Munich-Style Red Cabbage with Apples (p. 218)
Ginger-Spiced Carrots (p. 219)
Queen's Speech Peach Trifle (p. 223)

Roasted Vegetables with Fresh Sage

Roasting vegetables makes them taste nutty and sweet. Sound like anybody you know? This is a different way to prepare a side dish and you'll find it a welcome change from the plain boiled veggies that often accompany holiday meals.

2 tbsp (30 mL) soft margarine
1 tbsp (15 mL) chopped fresh sage
1 clove garlic, minced
1/2 pound (225 g) Brussels sprouts
1/2 pound (225 g) parsnips, peeled and cut in
  2-inch (5 cm) pieces
4 oz (112 g) baby carrots
1 small butternut squash, peeled, seeded and cut
  in 2-inch (5 cm) pieces

Preheat oven to 375°F (190°C).

   Melt the margarine in a small saucepan, then stir in the sage and garlic. Put all the vegetables in a large roasting pan and pour margarine mixture over. Toss to coat vegetables evenly. Bake, uncovered, for 25 to 30 minutes or until vegetables are tender, stirring and turning occasionally to allow the veggies to brown evenly without sticking.

Sweet and Aromatic Pumpkin Bread Pudding

Serves 12
Per serving:
Calories: 160
Fat: 2 g

Fragrant bread pudding is the ultimate comfort food, and the pumpkin adds a true seasonal flavor that could bump pumpkin pie off your menu for good. Add a dollop of low-fat whipped topping and you're in pumpkin paradise.

> 3 cups (750 mL) skim milk
> 1 cup (250 mL) packed brown sugar
> 1 tsp (5 mL) cinnamon
> 1 tsp (5 mL) vanilla
> 1/2 tsp (2 mL) nutmeg
> 1 egg
> 2 egg whites
> 1 14-oz (398 mL) can pumpkin
> 6 cups (1.5 mL) stale bread cubes, cut 1-inch
>   (2.5 cm) thick
> 1/2 cup (125 mL) raisins
> 1/2 cup (125 mL) slivered almonds

Preheat oven to 350°F (180°C).

Spray a 10-inch (25 cm) non-stick springform pan with cooking spray. Mix the milk, sugar, cinnamon, vanilla, nutmeg, egg, egg whites and pumpkin together in a large bowl. Add the bread cubes, raisins and almonds and combine well. Let the mixture stand for 10 minutes. Pour it into the prepared pan and bake for 60 to 90 minutes or until knife inserted in center comes out clean. Let stand 10 minutes and release sides of springform pan. Serve warm with low-fat whipped topping.

Serves 8

Per serving:

Calories: 130
Fat: 0.3 g

Suave Poached Pears with Blackberry Sauce

Pears gently poached in white wine are such an elegant dessert that we wanted to include them to give you a fancy option for your holiday spread.

> 8 pears, peeled (stems left on)
> 2 cups (500 mL) white wine
> 2 cups (500 mL) water
> 2 cups (500 mL) non-fat plain yogurt
> 1/2 cup (125 mL) blackberry preserves
> 1 tsp (5 mL) almond extract
> mint sprigs for garnish

In a large, deep saucepan, poach the pears in barely simmering wine and water for 8 to 10 minutes until tender but still firm. Remove them from the liquid with a slotted spoon and let drain on paper towels.

In a bowl, combine the yogurt, preserves and extract. Put a small amount of the yogurt mixture on each of 8 dessert plates and spread it out with the back of a spoon. Stand a pear on each plate on top of the sauce, and drizzle a little more of the mixture down the side of the pears. Garnish with a mint sprig.

The Skinny on Cooking With Wine

Cooking with wine adds very few calories and lots of big taste. But if you don't care to use vino, here are some substitutions that are easy to make. The taste won't be the same, however.

1. For white wine: chicken stock, vegetable stock or veggie juice
2. For red wine: beef stock, tomato juice
3. For Marsala or Port: stock or vegetable juice in savory recipes and fruit juice concentrates for desserts
4. Fruit liqueurs: fruit juice concentrates, lemon or orange peel, or vanilla
5. Brandy or rum: fruit juice concentrates or puréed fruit in dessert recipes

Chapter 10

Multi-Cultural Holiday Spread

Menu

Opa! Greek Dolmathes
Luscious Maritime Crab Bisque
Summer Fruit-Spinach Salad with Raspberry Vinaigrette
Holiday Smoked Trout with Lime Mayonnaise
Steve s Beef Tenderloin on Herb Biscuits with Horseradish Sauce
Munich-Style Red Cabbage with Apples
Ginger-Spiced Carrots
Over Ome Roasted Leg of Lamb
Aunt Sadie s Potato Knishes
Queen s Speech Peach Trifle
Caribbean Rum Bread Pudding

Introduction

We are blessed in Canada with a rich multi-cultural society which, thankfully, spills over onto the dinner table. You can eat your way around the world in most cities and, while it's delicious, it's also a great way to end up with a globe-sized girth.

We decided to bring the best from other countries' kitchens into ours for our holiday spread, adapting the recipes to trim fat and calories, but keeping the unique and exotic flavors. This is a spread you can lay on during any season, but we chose festive colors and themes to make it perfect for December entertaining, no matter what you're celebrating.

It's the people around the table who make your holiday gathering special. If you're like Wendy, and your friends and family live far away, coming together for a celebration spread makes the meal truly exceptional.

While you are discovering your own special holiday memories at this time of year, we hope some of them will come from this spread, as you share good food with the people you care about. For perhaps the first time, New Year's won't mean that you're doomed to start yet another diet the next day. You'll already be at a healthy weight, feeling fit and fine. This year, January will be full of possibilities, and the knowledge that you spent an entire year spreading yourself thin.

And just to be sure you, the head chef, get to enjoy every moment of the holiday feast, Barb is going to share her secret for keeping it simple and the day fun. Rent. Everything. From the dishes (who has dishes for 15 people?) to napkins, glasses, silver, you name it. It goes on the table from the box, then right back in that box to be returned after the holiday. No worries, and no washing up required. "It cost me $70 to rent everything, including the coffee urn," our clever Barb crows.

Think of it as our holiday gift to you.

Your lean body, healthy heart and fabulous, positive outlook are your gifts to yourself. Enjoy them all in great health and happiness.

♼ Cocktails

That magic time after the table is cleared and the kids are tucked in to dream their special dreams, when the world seems at peace, you toss another log on the fire, sink back into the sofa cushions and sip and savor this after-dinner treat.

After Dinner Coffee

1 oz (25 mL) Amaretto
1 oz (25 mL) Bailey's Irish Cream
fresh brewed coffee
real whipped cream, flavored with Kahlua
   instead of sugar or vanilla
shaved chocolate garnish

Pour Amaretto and Bailey's into a glass coffee mug. Top with coffee and low-fat whipped cream. Garnish with shaved chocolate.

Wine Suggestions
Pinot Grigio

Music Picks

 From Wendy

Natalie Cole, *Holly and Ivy*. Warner.

From Barb

José Carreras, Placido Domingo and Luciano Pavarotti, *Christmas Favourites*. Sony.

Makes 24 rolls

**Per serving
(4 rolls):**

**Calories: 98
Fat: trace**

Opa! Greek Dolmathes

These traditional Greek mezes, or appetizers, are delightful little packages wrapped in vine leaves. They're delicious hot or cold.

> **24 grape leaves, preserved in brine**
> **1 cup (250 mL) cooked white rice**
> **1 onion, finely diced**
> **1/2 tsp (2 mL) dried dill**
> **2 tsp (10 mL) dried oregano**
> **1/4 cup (50 mL) currants**
> **juice of 1 whole lemon**
> **non-fat yogurt**

Drain brine from the grape leaves (you'll find them in jars in the pickle section of your market) and put leaves in a colander. Rinse them very well with warm water and lay them out flat on paper towels to drain.

Combine the cooked rice, onion, dill, oregano and currants and mix well.

Place about 2 teaspoons (10 mL) of the rice filling on each leaf and roll it up like a burrito by first folding up the bottom edge, then fold the sides in, and roll. Place the rolls in a vegetable steamer basket and sprinkle the lemon juice over them. Put a heavy plate on top of the rolls to weigh them down and keep them from unrolling. Place the basket in a large pot of boiling water then reduce heat and simmer for 45 minutes, checking occasionally. Water should just cover the rolls. Remove the steamer basket from water and drain rolls well. Place on a serving platter and serve at room temperature with non-fat yogurt.

Luscious Maritime Crab Bisque

Serves 4

Per serving:

Calories: 257
Fat: 2 g

Smooth as silk, lavishly flavored with crab, tarragon and brandy, this rose-hued soup will simply wow your guests.

2 tsp (10 mL) olive oil
1 onion, finely chopped
3 cloves garlic, minced
2 carrots, sliced thinly
3 tbsp (45 mL) brandy
1/4 cup (50 mL) white wine
12 oz (340 g) crabmeat, fresh cooked or canned
2 cups (500 mL) vegetable broth
2 tbsp (30 mL) tomato paste
1/2 tsp (2 mL) dried tarragon
2 cups (500 mL) evaporated skim milk
salt and pepper
fresh chopped chives
pinch of cayenne pepper

In a large saucepan, heat the oil over medium heat. Add the onion and garlic and cook, stirring, until softened but not brown, about 5 minutes. Add the carrots and cook an additional 5 minutes, stirring frequently.

Remove the pan from heat and add the brandy. Return the pan to the heat and cook for 2 minutes. Add the wine and cook, stirring, until liquid is reduced, about 2 minutes. Stir in the crabmeat. If using canned, make sure you have rinsed it well and picked it over for shell bits and tendons. Add the broth, tomato paste and tarragon. Reduce heat and simmer, covered, for 5 minutes. Stir in the evaporated milk and bring to boil for 1 minute. Transfer the soup to a food processor or blender and purée until smooth. Season with salt and pepper and ladle into 4 soup bowls. Garnish with the chives and cayenne.

Summer Fruit-Spinach Salad with Raspberry Vinaigrette

Serves 4

Per serving:

Calories: 93
Fat: 1.5 g

Few things make more of a splash on a winter holiday table than the ripe, sweet fruits of summer. These days, it's easy to find these lovely fruits in northern climates when they're out of season. This salad looks as wonderful as it tastes, a festive red and green delight.

5 cups (1.25 L) fresh spinach, washed well
6 large strawberries, washed, hulled and sliced
2 kiwis, peeled and sliced

Dressing:
2 tbsp (30 mL) canola oil
1/4 cup (50 mL) vegetable stock
2 tbsp (30 mL) raspberry vinegar
2 tbsp (30 mL) honey
1 1/2 tbsp (20 mL) Dijon mustard
1 clove garlic, minced
2 tbsp (30 mL) skim milk
salt and pepper to taste

In a large salad bowl, combine the spinach, strawberries and kiwi. In a container with a tight-fitting lid, combine all dressing ingredients and shake well. Refrigerate for 30 minutes before serving. Toss with the greens and fruit and serve. Any leftover dressing can be stored in the refrigerator for up to 1 week.

Serves 4

Per serving:

Calories: 88
Fat: 3 g

Holiday Smoked Trout with Lime Mayonnaise

A very classy dish that is sure to impress.

> **1 to 3 smoked trout, total weight**
> **12 oz (375 g)**
> **fresh parsley and lemon wedges**

Bone and skin the trout, removing head and tail. You may put the fish back together to serve "whole," or divide into smaller segments. Place it on a platter and garnish with parsley and lemon. Serve lime mayonnaise on the side.

Serves 4

**Per serving
(1 tbsp/15 mL):**

Calories: 16
Fat: 0.5 g

Lime Mayonnaise

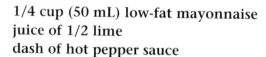

1/4 cup (50 mL) low-fat mayonnaise
juice of 1/2 lime
dash of hot pepper sauce

Whisk all the ingredients together. Chill. Serve with smoked trout.

Steve's Beef Tenderloin on Herb Biscuits with Horseradish Sauce

Serves 8

Per serving:

Calories: 212
Fat: 7 g

All hail Steve, king of the barbecue. This guy knows his way around a tenderloin. Although he'd probably stand knee-deep in snow to grill this delicious dish, we've adapted this Steve specialty to come up with a much more comfy oven-cooked method.

2 lb (1 kg) beef tenderloin, trimmed of all fat
1 1/2 cups (375 mL) white wine
2 tbsp (30 mL) soy sauce
2 cloves garlic, minced
1 onion, chopped
freshly ground pepper

In a shallow baking dish, mix the wine, soy sauce, garlic, onion and pepper. Place the tenderloin in the marinade and refrigerate for 1 hour, turning once or twice.

Preheat oven to 500°F (260°C). Place the tenderloin in a roasting pan and put it in the oven for 15 minutes. Turn the oven off and leave tenderloin in for 15 more minutes. Remove the beef from the oven and let it stand 5 minutes before carving. It will be medium-rare.

To serve, place a slice of tenderloin on one half of a herb biscuit (see page 216), drizzle a little of the horseradish sauce (see page 217) on top and place the other half of the biscuit beside it on the plate.

Parsleyed Biscuits for Beef Tenderloin

1 2/3 cups (425 mL) all-purpose flour
2 tsp (10 mL) granulated sugar
1 1/2 tsp (7 mL) baking powder
1/2 tsp (1 mL) baking soda
1/4 tsp (1 mL) salt
1 tbsp (15 mL) chopped fresh dill
1 tbsp (15 mL) chopped fresh parsley
2 tbsp (30 mL) soft margarine
2/3 cup (150 mL) buttermilk
2 tbsp (30 ml) olive oil

Preheat oven to 450°F (230°C).

Spray a baking sheet with cooking spray. In a large bowl, combine the flour, sugar, baking powder, soda and salt. Stir in the herbs. Using a pastry blender or two knives, cut in the margarine until mixture resembles coarse crumbs. Pour in the buttermilk and oil and stir to combine. Add a little more buttermilk if mixture is too dry.

Turn dough out on a lightly floured board and roll out to a 1/2-inch (1 cm) thickness. Using a 3-inch (7.5 cm) cookie cutter, or a drinking glass, cut dough into rounds. Place on baking sheet and bake for 10 to 12 minutes or until golden brown. Cut in half and place on a dinner plate. Top with beef tenderloin and horseradish sauce.

Horseradish Sauce for Beef Tenderloin

Makes 1¹/₄ cups
(300 mL)

Per serving
(1 tbsp/15 mL):

Calories: 8
Fat: trace

2 tbsp (30 mL) horseradish
1 cup (250 mL) plain non-fat yogurt
2 tbsp (30 mL) skim milk
1/2 tsp (2 mL) dried dill
salt and pepper to taste

Combine all ingredients and mix well. Refrigerate until ready to serve. Top each slice of tenderloin with sauce.

Serves 6

Per serving:

Calories: 109
Fat: 1 g

Munich-Style Red Cabbage with Apples

This delightful German dish tastes terrific and looks lovely with its soft burgundy color. Perfect for a holiday spread.

1 head red cabbage, about 1 1/2 lb (750 g), cored and thickly sliced
2 Granny Smith apples, peeled, cored and grated
1 tbsp (15 mL) brown sugar
1 tbsp (15 mL) red wine vinegar
2 tbsp (30 mL) all-purpose flour
salt and pepper to taste
1 cup (250 mL) red wine or apple juice

In a large non-aluminum saucepan, combine the cabbage, apples, sugar, vinegar, flour, salt and pepper. Bring to a boil over high heat. Reduce heat, cover and simmer for 30 minutes, stirring occasionally, until cabbage is tender.

Ginger-Spiced Carrots

Serves 8

Per serving:

Calories: 44

Fat: 1.5 g

We adore that Ginger, the original Spice Girl. And what she does to carrots is pure magic.

> 1 tbsp (15 mL) soft margarine
> 4 cups (1 L) sliced carrots
> 2 tsp (10 mL) lemon juice
> 2 tsp (10 mL) grated lemon zest
> 1 tsp (5 mL) fresh grated ginger

Over medium heat, melt the margarine in a large skillet. Add the carrots, lemon juice, zest and ginger. Stir to combine. Reduce heat to low. Cover and sauté for about 20 minutes until tender, stirring frequently and adding water if necessary.

Over 'Ome Roasted Leg of Lamb

A juicy leg of lamb, roasted to perfection, just like they do for Christmas lunch in Britain.

> 1 tsp (5 mL) soft margarine
> 2 cloves garlic, minced
> 1/3 cup (75 mL) finely chopped onion
> 3/4 cup (175 mL) bread crumbs
> 1/4 cup (50 mL) chopped parsley
> 1/3 cup (75 mL) vegetable broth
> 1 2 1/2 to 3-pound (1 to 1.5 kg) leg of lamb,
>   deboned, excess fat trimmed
> 1/3 cup (75 mL) red wine
> 1/3 cup (75 mL) beef or chicken stock

Preheat oven to 375°F (190°C).

In a large non-stick skillet, melt the margarine. Add the garlic and onion and sauté over medium heat for 5 minutes. Add bread crumbs, parsley and broth and mix well, adding more broth if mixture is too dry.

Place lamb in a roasting pan and pat bread crumb mixture evenly over the top. Pour the wine and stock into the bottom of the pan and cover pan with aluminum foil. Roast for 20 minutes. Uncover and roast for 15 to 20 minutes more until a meat thermometer reads 140°F (60°C) for rare, or cook until desired doneness.

Aunt Sadie's Potato Knishes

Serves 8

Per serving:

Calories: 175
Fat: 2 g

Knishes are traditional Jewish fare, although they're not specifically a holiday dish. Still, they're popular at any time of year, including Chanukkah. We've made them light and fluffy, a perfect addition to our spread.

> 4 large potatoes, peeled and diced
> 1 tbsp (15 mL) olive oil
> 1 onion, minced
> 2 cloves garlic, minced
> 2 egg whites, lightly beaten
> 1 tbsp (15 mL) chopped fresh parsley
> 1 tbsp (15 mL) chopped fresh chives
> 1 tbsp (15 mL) chopped fresh oregano
> 1 tbsp (15 mL) chopped fresh basil
> 1 tbsp (15 mL) chopped fresh thyme
> 1 tbsp (15 mL) paprika
> salt and pepper to taste
> 1 1/4 cups (300 mL) all-purpose flour

Put the potatoes in a large saucepan and cover with cold water. Bring to a boil, lower heat and simmer for 10 minutes or until potatoes are tender. Drain and place in a large bowl. Set aside.

Heat the oil in a large non-stick skillet. Add the onion and sauté over medium-low heat for 5 minutes. Add the garlic and sauté another 10 minutes, stirring frequently.

Set aside. When cool, stir in the egg whites, herbs and paprika.

Mash the potatoes until fairly smooth. Add the onion mixture, salt and pepper.

Stir in 1/4 cup (60 mL) of the flour until you have a mixture that is a little sticky, but holds together.

Preheat oven to 350°F (180°C).

Place the remaining 1 cup (250 mL) flour on a plate. Form the potato mixture into slightly rectangular patties 1-inch (2.5 cm) thick by 3 inches (7.5 cm) long. Dredge with the flour, shaking off excess. Place patties on a non-stick baking sheet that has been lightly sprayed with cooking spray. Bake for 35 to 40 minutes until nicely browned and heated through. Serve immediately.

Queen's Speech Peach Trifle

Serves 8

Per serving:

Calories: 209
Fat: 1 g

Every Christmas Day, Queen Elizabeth II makes a speech to her subjects. In some Canadian homes, it's become a tradition to gather round the TV and watch the speech. Even if it's not at yours, this trifle should be. Enjoy this new, light spin on a traditional English pudding.

> 1 cup (250 mL) low- or non-fat vanilla yogurt
> 1 package vanilla pudding mix
> 2 cups (500 mL) skim milk
> 1/3 cup (80 mL) raspberry jam
> 1 tbsp (15 mL) dry sherry
> 4 1/2 cups (1.1 L) angel food cake, cut into cubes
> 1 can sliced peaches in juice, drained, 3 slices
>   reserved for garnish
> mint sprigs

Pour the yogurt into a coffee filter set in a colander over a bowl and let drain for 5 to 10 minutes.

In a large bowl, whisk together the pudding mix and milk until well blended. Add the drained yogurt and stir to combine. Set aside.

In a small bowl, mix the jam and sherry. Set aside.

In a large deep glass bowl, arrange half of the cake cubes. Spread half of the pudding mixture over them. Spoon half the jam mixture over the pudding, and top with half the peaches. Repeat layers in the same order with remaining ingredients. Garnish with the reserved peach slices and mint.

For a change, this trifle is also delicious when made with a 15-ounce (425 g) package of frozen unsweetened raspberries, sweetened with 1 tablespoon (15 mL) granulated sugar, instead of the peaches.

Caribbean Rum Bread Pudding

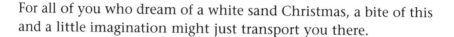

For all of you who dream of a white sand Christmas, a bite of this and a little imagination might just transport you there.

> 1/3 cup (75 mL) light rum
> 1/2 cup (125 mL) raisins
> 3 cups (750 mL) evaporated skim milk
> 1 cup (250 mL) egg substitute
> 2/3 cup (150 mL) packed brown sugar
> 1 tsp (5 mL) vanilla extract
> 3/4 cup (175 mL) stale french bread, cut in cubes
> boiling water

Preheat oven to 350°F (180°C).

In a small bowl, combine the rum and raisins. Set aside for 10 minutes.

In a large bowl, whisk together the evaporated milk, egg substitute, sugar and vanilla. Stir in the raisins and rum. Add the bread cubes, stir to combine well and set aside for 20 minutes.

Pour mixture into a non-stick loaf pan. Place loaf pan in a large roasting pan that has been set into the preheated oven. Pour boiling water into the roasting pan until it reaches about halfway up the sides of the loaf pan. Bake for about 55 minutes, or until pudding is set in the center. Remove from the oven and let cool in the loaf pan.

Turn pudding out onto a serving plate and slice.

Index

focaccia, rosemary, 146–147
sticky, 58

Bread pudding
   pumpkin, 203
   rum, Caribbean, 224
Broccoli
   in broccomoli, 122
   soup, creamy, 192
   in teriyaki salad, 77
Broccomoli, 122
Bruschetta, 148
Buffet tips, 190
Burger(s)
   chicken, 105
   tip, 104
   turkey, 104

C

Cabbage
   with apples, Munich-style,
   218
   coleslaw, 177
   in teriyaki salad, 77
Cake(s)
   chocolate, mocha madness,
   71–72
   chocolate, with raspberry
   sauce, 26–28
   strawberry, short-, 110
Candy cravings, how to banish,
   167
Caribbean Rum Bread Pudding,
   224
Carrots
   ginger-spiced, 219
   in Waldorf slaw, 78
Casserole(s)
   eggplant parmigiana, 153
   lasagne, 151–152
   scalloped potatoes, 65
   sweet potato, 200
Caviar-Stuffed Cherry Tomatoes,
   38
Cheese(s)
   football, herbed, 168
   mozzarella-tomato salad, 141

yogo, 14
Cherries jubilee, sinful, 25

Chicken
   black tie, 19–20
   burgers, 105
   dredging mixture, 19
   Gina Lollobrigida, 157
   mole, 131
   roasted, with figs, 45
   satays, 98–99
   southern unfried, 82
   strips, 169–170
Chicken Mole, 131
Chili
   con carne, 132–133
   vegetarian, 175–176
Chilies, varieties and potency,
   122
Chill-Out Chili, 175–176
Chips
   pita, 95
   potato, 167
   tortilla, 166
Chocolate
   cake, with raspberry sauce,
   26–28
   cake, mocha madness, 71–72
   dip, for fruit, 49
   -mousse martini, 35
   syrup, nutritional information, 27
Chocolate Mousse Martini, 35
Chutney
   jump-up, 64
   Mum's, 85
Cider, spiced apple, 188
Cinnamon crispas, 134–135
Classic Creamy Coleslaw, 177
Classic Martini, 33
Classic Roast Turkey, 194–197
Cluck It Up Chicken Burgers,
   105
Cobb salad, 102–103
Cobbler, peachy, 70
Cocktail(s)
   aperitif, St. Raphael, 139
   Hoss's morning after, 54

kir royale, 10
   sea breeze, 94
   see also Beverages; Margaritas;
   Martinis
Coffee
   after dinner, 208
   in mocha madness chocolate
   cake, 71–72
Colds, foods to help relieve, 119
Coleslaw, classic creamy, 177
Commemorativo Margarita, 116
Condiments
   broccomoli, 122
   chutney
      jump-up, 64
      Mum's, 85
   horseradish sauce, 217
   jam, onion, 96
   ketchup, cranberry, 106
   mayonnaise, lime, 214
   mustard sauce, 63
   pickled beets, 108
   pickles, pucker up, 84
   relish
      cranberry-orange, 198
      pepper, rainbow, 107
   salsa, 121
   see also Pesto
Cookies
   apricot biscotti, 160
   date, 181
   midnight raid, 225
Cooking liquid, reducing
   technique, 6
Cool 'n' caliente salad dressing,
   123
Corn and pepper sauté, mosaic,
   129
Cornbread, jalapeño, 126
Couscous, Moroccan delight, 22
Cozumel Crunch Crackers,
   118–119
Crab and Artichoke Tartlets, 191
Crab bisque, 211–212
Crackers, Cozumel crunch,
   118–119
Cranberry(ies)
   cocktails, 33–34, 94, 139

ketchup, 106
relish, -orange, 198
Cranberry Ketchup, 106
Creamy Dream of Broccoli
Soup, 192
Crispas, with strawberries,
134–135
Curry Some Flavor Turkey Pitas,
81

D

Date cookies, 181
Decadent Martini, 35
Decadent Roast Chicken with
Figs, 45
Dessert(s)
Betty, blueberry, 90
bread pudding
pumpkin, 203
rum, Caribbean, 224
bread, sticky, 58
cherries, jubilee, 25
cobbler, peach, 70
crisp, apple, 182–183
ice, lemon, 109
parfaits, ambrosia, 50
pears, poached, 204
pineapple, grilled, 111
sorbet, nectarine, 159
trifle, peach, 223
see also Cakes; Cookies
Devilish Raspberry Sauce for
Angelic
Chocolate Cake, 28
Diets that don't work, 111
Dip(s)
artichoke, 37
bean, 120
broccomoli, 122
chocolate, for fruit, 49
cool 'n' caliente, 123
for fruit kebobs, 88–89
mustard, 12
onion jam, for pita chips, 96
plum sauce, 170
raspberry-poppyseed, 88
salsa, 121

sour cream, for fruit kebobs, 89
spinach, 190
Dive-In Pita Chips, 95
Dolmathes, Greek, 210
Dredging
mixture for chicken, 19
technique, 6
Drunken Fruit, 56

E

Eggplant parmigiana, 153
Elegant Pork Tenderloin, 21
Erotic Ambrosia Parfaits, 50
Exercise program tips
for weight training, 11
for working out with children,
140
Exotic Herbed Orzo, 46

F

50-Yard Line Apple Crisp,
182–183
Fads, what's in, what's out, 38
Fajitas, shrimp, 127–128
Fancy Greens with Pine Nuts
and Balsamic
Dressing, 193
Fat
-burning formula, weight
training, 11
-cutting tips, 83
skimming technique, 6
substitutions for cutting, 183
First Down Roasted Garlic and
Tomato
Pizza, 179
Fish
cooking technique, 61
see also specific types; Seafood
Florentine Stuffed Shells, 66
Flour dredging technique, 6
Focaccia, rosemary, 146–147
Foods that fill you up, 47
French toast, twisted, 67
Fries, spicy, 174
Frittata, rainbow pepper, 59

Fruit
chocolate dipped, 49
chutney, 64, 85
kebobs, with dipping sauces,
87–89
parfaits, ambrosia, 50
salad
drunken, 56
with spinach, 213
slaw, Waldorf
see also specific fruits; Desserts
Fruit Kebobs with Two Dipping
Sauces, 87–89

G

Garlic
potatoes, smashed, 47
roasted, 20, 179
with chicken or vegetables,
44
pizza, with tomatoes, 179
sauce, sweet Polynesian, 99
Garlic Smashed Potatoes, 47
Get Lucky Pasta, 43–44
Gina Lollobrigida Chicken, 157
Ginger-Spiced Carrots, 219
Go Wild Rice Stuffing, 195
Gobble Gobble Stuffed Squash,
201
Grape leaf dolmathes, 210
Gravy, turkey, 197
Greens, see specific types; Salads
Grill 'Em Danno Grilled
Pineapple, 110

H

Ham, old-fashioned, 62–63
Hearty Black Bean Soup with
Tortilla
Strips, 124–125
Herb(s)
basil, pesto, 154
marjoram, substitute for
oregano, 22
oregano, substitute for, 22
in orzo, exotic, 46

Oregano substitute, 22
Orzo, exotic herbed, 46

Over 'Ome Roasted Leg of
    Lamb, 220
Oysters, rockin' Rockefeller,
    39–40

P

Parfaits, erotic ambrosia, 50
Parsleyed Biscuits for Beef
    Tenderloin, 216
Parties, 10 best places for, 99
Pasta
    angel hair, in get lucky-,
        43–44
    lasagne, 151–152
    orzo, herbed, 46
    salad, tuna, 79
    shells, Florentine stuffed, 66
Peach(es)
    cobbler, 69
    trifle, 223
Peachy Cobbler, 69
Pears, poached with blackberry
    sauce, 204
Pepper(s)
    in Cobb salad, 102–103
    and corn sauté, 129
    frittata, rainbow, 59
    hot, varieties and potency, 120
    marinated, roasted, 144
    pesto, roasted red, 155
    relish, rainbow, 107
    roasted, 101
        and marinated, 144
        in pesto, 155
    in veggie roll-ups, 80
Pesto
    basil, 154
    pepper, roasted, 155
    pizza, with shrimp, 149–150
    Santa Fe, 155
    sundried tomato, 149
    variations, low-fat, 154–155
Pickled beets, 108
Pickles, pucker up, 84
Pineapple, grilled, 111

Pita(s)
    chips, 95
    turkey, curried, 81
Pizza
    garlic and tomato, roasted, 179
    mushroom and spinach, 180
    ordering, what to avoid, 150
    pesto, sundried tomato,
        149–150
    shrimp and tomato pesto,
        149–150
    spinach and mushroom, 180
    toppings, low-fat suggestions,
        180
Pizza dough
    basic, 178–179
    using focaccia for, 150
Plum Sauce, 170
Polynesian Sweet Garlic Sauce, 99
Poppyseed-raspberry dip for
    fruit
    kebobs, 88
Pork
    ham, old-fashioned, 62–63
    tenderloin, elegant, 21
Potato(es)
    baked, magic, 23
    chips, 167
    fries, spicy, 174
    knishes, 221–222
    mashed, buttermilk, 199
    oven-fried, 174
    salad, 100–101
    scalloped, 65
    smashed, garlic, 47
    sweet, casserole, 200
Poultry see Chicken, Turkey
Pucker Up Pickles, 84
Pumpkin bread pudding, 203

Q

Quarterback Chicken Strips,
    169–170
Queen's Speech Peach Trifle,
    223

R

Rainbow Pepper Frittata, 59
Rainbow Pepper Relish, 107
Raspberry
    -poppyseed dip for fruit
        kebobs, 88
    sauce, devilish, 28
    vinaigrette, 213
Raspberry-Poppyseed Dip, 88
Reducing liquids, technique, 6
Relish
    cranberry-orange, 198
    pepper, rainbow, 107
Rice
    spicy, 130
    stuffing, 195
    wild, stuffing, 195
Rich Turkey Gravy, 197
Roasted Asparagus, 24
Roasted Vegetables with Fresh
    Sage, 202
Rock and Roma Lasagne,
    151–152
Rockin' Oysters Rockefeller,
    39–40
Roll-ups
    lasagne, 151–152
    veggie, Santa Fe, 80
Romaine
    in Caesar salad, 41
    in Cobb salad, 102–103
Rosemary Focaccia, 146–147
Rosy Roasted Red Pepper Pesto,
    155
Rum bread pudding, 224

S

Saintly Scalloped Potatoes, 65
Salad(s)
    -bar choices, good and bad, 60
    Caesar, 41
    Cobb, 102–103
    coleslaw, 177